R. T. Kendall is a giant of the faith and has demonstrated a life of faithfulness. In *It Ain't Over Till It's Over* he draws on his life experience and leads the reader to place their faith in God, reminding them that "it ain't over till it's over." This book will challenge you, regardless of your age or stage, to finish well.

—ED STETZER

WWW.EDSTETZER.COM

These pages reveals R. T. Kendall as a man who truly loves God with all his heart, soul, might, and mind. Accordingly I am very proud to be among the beneficiaries of his love. He fervently hopes that I will share the fullness of his faith, which actually divides us, while I am happy for each of us to live devotedly according to our different faiths (my understanding of Habakkuk 2:4) but still united as the great Jewish philosopher Martin Buber put it, by "a book and a hope, and that is no small thing."

—RABBI SIR DAVID ROSEN

For a Christian, life is full of preachers, sermons, and books. Let's be honest. The fact is that many of them are quite boring. Since I was a teenager still at school, my father would tell me about one preacher who was different, one preacher you could listen to who was not boring, one preacher you could trust with every word because he was rather "sound." Years later he would become a good friend, and I would become famous as the man who took him to see another friend of mine—President Yasser Arafat. It has been an incredible journey we have taken together over the years, but it has not finished yet. He may be retired, he may have left his famous Westminster Chapel, but he has not stopped, and God has not finished with him yet. As you read this book, you will see that R. T. Kendall is not retired but re-fired. Re-fired with the glorious anointing of the Spirit of the living God. As you study this book, you too will have the opportunity to have

D0003046

your faith, life, and trust in the Almighty re-fired. This book out of his many writings is an absolute must. Because "it ain't over till it's over."

—REV. CANON DR. ANDREW P. B. WHITE
VICAR EMERITUS OF BAGHDAD

I hope this book will help many people.

—YOGI BERRA
MAJOR LEAGUE BASEBALL HALL OF FAME INDUCTEE AND
ALL-CENTURY TEAM MEMBER

Dr. R. T. Kendall has written a masterpiece of theology, inspiration, and evangelism. I believe it is his crowning work. His words are so needed in people's lives and in the church today. This book will be a treasure for generations to come should Jesus tarry. He has been so very dear to my heart for about thirty five years. This is Kendall at his best.

—ARTHUR BLESSITT
LUKE 18:1

When you read RT's books, you always come out with gems that are so applicable to your life and certainly a revelation of the Holy Spirit. For example, when he writes in his book, "Unanswered prayer is an opportunity to get to know God's ways." That stands out to me. We don't always look at things like that.

I like the way RT presents God's timing also because I am an impatient person. I want to pray and see it answered in the next thirty seconds. But God has a plan, and RT shows it brilliantly and spiritually in his book, *It Ain't Over Till It's Over*. I recommend it wholeheartedly. I read it all, every page, and felt so blessed, encouraged, and provoked to follow God's Word and the Holy Spirit.

—DR. MARILYN HICKEY
PRESIDENT, MARILYN HICKEY MINISTRIES

Our good friend R. T. Kendall has done it again! Blending sound theology with genuineness and practical applications. A helpful tool for those committed to staying in the game and finishing strong! I continue to be enriched and blessed with RT's insights and teachings and value this wonderful gift to the body of Christ.

—Paul Berube
Senior minister, Gate City Church
Nashua, New Hampshire

The older I get, the more important the concept of hope is to me. Outside of Scripture there is no book I know of that anchors my soul in God-filled hope like this excellent work by R. T. Kendall.

—Stephen Chitty
Lead pastor, Christian Life Church
Columbia, South Carolina

I was blessed to witness two of God's servants meet for the first time: baseball great Yogi Berra, and renowned theologian Dr. R. T. Kendall. From that meeting came the Hall of Famer's endorsement of *It Ain't Over Till It's Over*. Not only an apt description of the Hall of Famer's indomitable spirit, but also of Dr. Kendall's biblically based explanation of how we all can "finish well," being admitted to the greatest Hall of Fame there is: heaven.

—James "JB" Brown
CBS NFL sportscaster

Again from the pen of R. T. Kendall comes this masterpiece that, in a broad sweep through life's vital subjects, we are introduced to a protocol for finishing this life well. This is an endeavor every one of us will consider, and this book will prove to be a helpful aid in the pursuit of such a finish.

—Charles Carrin
—Jack Taylor

It Ain't Over Till It's Over exudes profound experience of Christ, proven spiritual truth, and ever-increasing knowledge of God. R. T. Kendall gives you all it takes to run humbly, yet confidently to the finishing line. No one, no matter how young or old, should be without this book.

—Rev. Colin Dye
Senior pastor, Kensington Temple
London, England

In a day when many have lost their way and are struggling to finish well, RT writes to inspire us to live lives of integrity as we prepare to step out of time and into eternity, and to give account of our lives to God. If you live right now, you'll be thankful you did and greatly blessed then.

—Grant Brewster
Pastor, Island Church
Bainbridge Island, Washington

Here is yet another in a long line of books from the prolific pen of R. T. Kendall. As Yogi Berra would say, "It is déjà vu all over again," in the sense that you know this volume, like all his others, is going to be theologically stimulating to your mind, passionately stirring to your heart, and in the end is going to move you to act on what you have read. I have known Kendall for almost four decades and consider him to be "closer than a brother." No one I know has a heart for genuine revival more than this time tested good and godly man. And, no one I know is finishing his own race any stronger than him. Kendall is walking, talking, living proof that "it ain't over till it's over"!

—O. S. Hawkins
Former minister,
First Baptist Church Dallas, Texas
President/CEO GuideStone Financial Resources

On a daily basis millions of "whys" rise up to heaven from many a prison of afflictions. In this unique book R. T. Kendall offers hope for persevering and never giving up. *It Ain't Over Till It's Over* is a desperately needed book, not only because it provides reasons for hope, but also because RT does something seldom a leader of his caliber offers—vulnerability. He opens his heart and reveals his own temptation to loss of hope, but then he also gives all of the glory to the Lord for persevering and subsequent victories. Read this book and soar on the wings of Christian hope.

—Dr. Michael Youssef
Senior minister, Church of the Apostles
Atlanta, Georgia

Congratulations to RT on his eightieth birthday. I hope he writes many more books, but should this be the last, it's a brilliant Last Will and Testament!

—Lyndon Bowring
CARE, London, England

IT AIN'T OVER TILL IT'S OVER

R.T. KENDALL

CHARISMA
HOUSE

Most CHARISMA HOUSE BOOK GROUP products are available at special quantity discounts for bulk purchase for sales promotions, premiums, fund-raising, and educational needs. For details, write Charisma House Book Group, 600 Rinehart Road, Lake Mary, Florida 32746, or telephone (407) 333-0600.

IT AIN'T OVER TILL IT'S OVER by R. T. Kendall
Published by Charisma House
Charisma Media/Charisma House Book Group
600 Rinehart Road
Lake Mary, Florida 32746
www.charismahouse.com

This book or parts thereof may not be reproduced in any form, stored in a retrieval system, or transmitted in any form by any means—electronic, mechanical, photocopy, recording, or otherwise—without prior written permission of the publisher, except as provided by United States of America copyright law.

Scripture quotations marked NIV are taken from the Holy Bible, New International Version®, NIV®. Copyright © 1973, 1978, 1984, 2011 by Biblica, Inc.™ Used by permission of Zondervan. All rights reserved worldwide. www.zondervan.com The "NIV" and "New International Version" are trademarks registered in the United States Patent and Trademark Office by Biblica, Inc.™

Scripture quotations marked ESV are from the Holy Bible, English Standard Version. Copyright © 2001 by Crossway Bibles, a division of Good News Publishers. Used by permission.

Scripture quotations marked KJV are from the King James Version of the Bible.

Scripture quotations marked MEV are taken from the Holy Bible, Modern English Version. Copyright © 2014 by Military Bible Association. Used by permission. All rights reserved.

Scripture quotations marked NKJV are taken from the New King James Version®. Copyright © 1982 by Thomas Nelson. Used by permission. All rights reserved.

Scripture quotations marked NIRV are taken from the Holy Bible, New International Reader's Version®. Copyright © 1996, 1998 1998, 2014 by Biblica. All rights reserved throughout the world. Used by permission of Biblica.

Scripture quotations marked NLT are from the Holy Bible, New Living Translation, copyright © 1996, 2004, 2007. Used by permission of Tyndale House Publishers, Inc., Wheaton, IL 60189. All rights reserved.

Copyright © 2015 by R. T. Kendall
All rights reserved

Cover design by Vincent Pirozzi
Design Director: Justin Evans

Visit the author's website at www.rtkendallministries.com.

Library of Congress Cataloging-in-Publication Data:
Kendall, R. T.
 It ain't over till it's over / by R.T. Kendall. -- First edition.
    pages cm
 Includes bibliographical references and index.
 ISBN 978-1-62998-600-5 (trade paper : alk. paper) -- ISBN 978-1-62998-601-2 (e-book)
 1. Perseverance (Ethics) 2. Christian life. 3. God (Christianity)--Faithfulness. I. Title.
 BV4647.P45K46 2015
 248.4--dc23
                                    2015014130

First edition

15 16 17 18 19 — 987654321
Printed in the United States of America

To Bill and Vivian

CONTENTS

PART I:
GOD'S WAYS

PART II:
JUMPING TO A CONCLUSION

PART III:
THE FAITHFULNESS OF GOD

SPECIAL
RECOMMENDATION

O NE SUNDAY AFTER church service RT, his wife, a
couple friends, and I jumped in a couple cars full of
excitement to go see the great Yogi Berra. Now I had known
Yogi for over twenty years, but for some in our group it would
be their first and only chance to meet Yogi. Now Yogi was getting up in age and physically had become weak. He was not the
same Yogi we had seen on TV commercials or for some in a
baseball uniform; no he had become so weak by now that RT
and I were the only visitors allowed to visit him that day. As we
sat with Yogi in his room, we knew by first appearance our visit
would be short. After about five minutes Yogi was spent. He
had had a rough night sleeping and needed to rest, but before
he lay down to rest he whispered something to me that was so
fitting to the title of the book. He said "I ain't got much time." I
looked at RT, and he had heard it too. I was stunned! What do
you do? We thought for sure he was saying, "That's it. I'm gonna
die!" Not only die but die that day! Well we prayed with Yogi,
thanked God for allowing us to be there that day, spoke for a
minute or two longer, and then said our good-byes. Good-byes

we thought were final. Good-bye to the great Yogi Berra! At least we thought! Well, that was months ago and so fitting to Yogi's life he's still kickin' to this day. Fitting to the book you might say. I think so because just as you will find in this book, as in life, I guess it really "ain't over till it's over"!

—Harold Reynolds
FOX Sports

FOREWORD

TWO YEARS AGO Dr. R. T. Kendall asked me to pray for him. His tone and facial expression changed from one of light-heartedness to a more somber, serious one, as he voiced this request. There are five levels of communication—level one being cliché and surface talk while the highest is level five. That is where deep, honest thoughts and private feelings are expressed. In an instant our conversation moved to a level five. My friend RT had asked me to: "Pray that I finish well."

At the time I was fifty years old; approximately thirty years his junior. I was humbled by his appeal; yet proud he asked *me*. After a few seconds I recognized what precipitated this unusual request. He was looking in his internal rearview mirror and was thankful to God for the rich journey of faith he'd successfully traversed. The joy of being married to his sweetheart, Louise, for more than fifty years, the twenty-five years of irreplaceable memories from pastoring the famed Westminster Chapel in London, to his being mentored by the prince of preachers, Dr. Martyn Lloyd-Jones. Each of these priceless experiences, not-withstanding the other vast ministry accomplishments, pro-vided a beautiful legacy that he did not want foiled by an unwise decision or momentary lapse in judgment in the winter years of his ministry. His successes were also a clear stepping-stone for younger ministers like me to walk upon. These treasures had to be safeguarded through prayer.

Dr. Kendall's request came from a deep place of introspection. He was looking ahead through the window of his soul to the time in which His Lord and Savior, Jesus Christ would call him home. My friend did not want anything up ahead to hinder him from answered prayers, victorious Christian living, and ultimately from finishing well. And, true to form, RT is not one to look for slick gimmicks or contemporary tactics devoid of sound orthodoxy or the Holy Spirit's power. Dr. Kendall is a man of prayer and a man dependent on prayer to secure God's promises, guidance, and strength.

Suffice it to say, I did not hesitate for a single moment to pray for him and continue to pray to this day that he finishes well. In fact, I've started to pray for myself in that same vein. I too want to finish well, having a life and ministry free of scandals, an unalterable love for the church, an evangelistic fervor for the lost, and a contagious love for God.

Aristotle said: "Man is a goal-seeking animal. His life only has meaning if he is reaching out and striving for his goals." This book embodies Dr. Kendall's noble goal to persevere in all things, and ultimately to finish his ministry *well*. This desire shows the character and the wisdom of the man. It also reflects his heart that says: A life well lived casts a huge shadow that's sure to impact coming generations for Christ.

Toward the end of Paul's ministry he proudly said to Timothy: "I have fought the good fight, I have finished the race, I have kept the faith" (2 Tim. 4:7, NKJV). In *It Ain't Over*

Till It's Over Dr. Kendall provides a contemporary road map showing us the rewards of perseverance in many areas of life and how we too can accomplish Paul's exemplary feat with our lives and ministries.

As you read this masterpiece, you will journey with Dr. Kendall across continents, many decades of ministry, and through tons of faith-building stories. As chapter builds upon chapter, you'll discover all the ways we are called to persevere in faith until God says, "It is finished." Each step along the way you will find yourself becoming more anchored in your faith while gaining confidence to say, "It ain't over till it's over!"

—DAVID D. IRELAND, PHD
SENIOR PASTOR, AUTHOR, *THE KNEELING WARRIOR*
WWW.DAVIDIRELAND.ORG

PREFACE

SOMEONE CAME UP to me a couple years ago and said, "It is so good to meet someone who has finished well." I tried to smile.

For several years I have envisioned writing a book on the general theme of finishing well, thinking I would do this with particular reference to my eightieth birthday in July 2015. I assumed I might be forgiven for writing on this subject at that age, although I could not be sure—even then—that I would truly finish well. So I wanted to call such a book, *It Ain't Over Till It's Over*, using one of Yogi Berra's most famous *Yogi-isms* (as they came to be called).

I also assumed that the book on finishing well might be a sequel to *In Pursuit of His Glory*, an autobiographical account of my twenty-five years at Westminster Chapel.[1] But at a meeting with my publisher and editor the idea was put to me to expand the present book to more than my own finishing well. Although I have included some anecdotes throughout the book, some of which have come out of the years since we left Westminster, "Finishing Well" ends up being only one chapter in the present book—right at the end.

In August 2012 as I was being driven to speak at Christ Church in Montclair, New Jersey, my driver commented: "Yogi Berra lives in this town."

I immediately replied, "I would really love to meet that man." An hour later in the pulpit I put a rather cheeky request to the people, although it was not my first visit there. I asked, "Does anybody here know Yogi Berra or where he lives?" No one in the congregation of several hundred apparently knew, although it was well known that he lived in the area. I later came to the conclusion that it was easier to meet the Pope than Yogi Berra!

Dr. David Ireland, the senior minister of Christ Church, later asked the television sportscaster Harold Reynolds, who is a member of his congregation, if he would pave the way for me to meet Yogi. It turned out that all roads led to David Kaplan, Yogi's close friend and director of the Yogi Berra Museum and Learning Center in Montclair. During this time I met James Brown, the CBS sportscaster known as JB. He and his wife, Dorothy, had come to hear me preach at The Cove in Asheville, North Carolina. JB and Harold Reynolds knew each other well. Therefore, through the influence of Dr. Ireland, JB, and Harold, David Kaplan was persuaded to let me meet Yogi.

In November 2013—some sixteen months after my efforts began, my son TR and I flew to New Jersey, and we met Yogi Berra. JB came from his home in Maryland to be present for the occasion. Yogi himself gave us a private tour of his museum— a wonderful honor. I then had time with Yogi alone. I talked to him about Jesus Christ and prayed with him. He graciously gave us permission to use the phrase, "It ain't over till it's over," for my book and even allowed us to use photographs taken of us together for the book.

Yogi Berra could not have known how vast the potential was for his remarkable comment. I have therefore used this phrase to embrace more possibilities than finishing well, but within the confines of biblical truth and sound theology. I will in any case close the book with my original goal—the need for all Christians, especially leaders, to finish well. My friend Lyndon Bowring visited the ailing John Stott only weeks before the legendary leader went to heaven a few years ago. John said to Lyndon, "Please pray that I will finish well." Amazing. Think of that. Even when near death one might still have the fear of not finishing well! After all, "It ain't over till it's over."

My warmest thanks to my publishers Steve and Joy Strang. How good God has been to me that in my retirement I could have the privilege of writing books published by them. I especially thank Tessie DeVore, executive vice president of Charisma Media Book Group, who first pointed out the many ways, "It ain't over till it's over," might be used! My thanks to Debbie Marrie for her continued encouragement, and to my editor, Barbara Dycus. Also thanks to Woodley Auguste for his wise input. I am so very grateful to my two British friends Rob Parsons and Lyndon Bowring for their prudent and helpful suggestions. Thank you, Dr. David Ireland, for writing the gracious foreword. My deepest gratitude, as always, is to my wife, Louise—my best friend and critic—for her support and input.

I pray this book will be a blessing to you as you read it.

—R. T. KENDALL
HENDERSONVILLE, TENNESSEE

INTRODUCTION

M Y FRIEND CHARLES Carrin shared this story with me:

> My wife's cousin had lymphoma thirty years ago. They did
> not use the phrase *stage four* cancer in those days, saying
> only that it was a dire emergency. Three days before his sur-
> gery I had a word of knowledge that he was healed. I abso-
> lutely knew it was so. He did not believe me, but they did
> more X-rays. On the day he was to enter Baptist Hospital
> in Atlanta, he was in the shower getting ready to go when
> the report came back the cancer was gone...Hallelujah!

In our last years at Westminster Chapel we regularly made
the anointing of oil available for the sick—according to James
5:14: "Is anyone among you sick? Let them call the elders of the
church to pray over them and anoint them with oil in the name
of the Lord." A Muslim woman named Miah came forward to
be prayed for. I had not seen her before, nor did I know the
nature of her illness. We merely prayed for her, anointing her
with oil. Months later she told me this story:

I had throat cancer. You prayed for me on a Sunday. The following Thursday I went into the hospital for surgery. They took one more X-ray. As I was lying on the operating table they came in and double-checked who I was and who the consulting doctor was. They simply told me there was no cancer and no need to operate. They sent me home.

Miah came to me the following weekend and said, "I want to convert." I shared the gospel with her. She received it gladly. I baptized her a few weeks later. She became a member of Westminster Chapel several months after that. She now lives in California and regularly keeps in touch with us.

Do you think it's *over* for you? Have you given up hope? Have you lost heart that your prayers will be answered? Have you given up on your dream that your deepest longing will be fulfilled?

Do you fear you are *finished*? That *it's over* for you?

If you have been asking questions such as these, this book is for you. It is my prayer that the Holy Spirit will convince you through the reading of this book that *it is not too late*.

I asked Yogi Berra when he first made the original comment, "It ain't over till it's over?"

"At Shea Stadium," he replied. It was *not* when he was the baseball catcher with the New York Yankees, but rather when he was the manager of the New York Mets years later. In July 1973 everything went wrong for the New York Mets. They were at the very bottom of the eastern division of the National League.

The owner of the Giants was planning to fire Yogi. A reporter said to him, "Is it all over, Yogi?"

Yogi replied, "It ain't over till it's over."

"It just rolled out," Yogi said to me. He had no idea this phrase would be used thousands and thousands of times since then. When the popular children's cartoon Yogi Bear was created, the phrase—along with other *Yogi-isms*—was often heard.

If you are an older American reader you will know exactly who Yogi Berra is. If not, allow me to introduce him—a phenomenal man. He quit school after the eighth grade (aged thirteen or fourteen) and became one of the greatest baseball players of all time. He was the New York Yankees's catcher for most of his career in baseball and is widely regarded as the greatest baseball catcher ever. He was named the Most Valuable Player in the American League three times. He appeared in twenty-one World Series, winning thirteen of them. He was inducted into the baseball Hall of Fame in 1972. He was also a journalist's dream, frequently mangling sentences that made no grammatical sense but which all somehow understood.

For my seventieth birthday my son, TR, gave me an autographed baseball of Yogi Berra with his handwriting, "It ain't over till it's over." He also gave me a plaque with several Yogi-isms, which we hung on the wall in our family room:

- "It's déjà vu all over again."
- "It gets late early out here."
- "You can observe a lot by watching."
- "The future isn't what it used to be."
- "Never answer an anonymous letter."
- "When you come to a fork in the road, take it!"
- "I didn't really say everything I said."

But his phrase, "It ain't over till it's over," became his best known. How many times has a baseball game seemed over—with fans leaving the stadium for their cars—when in the ninth inning with the score 3–0 in favor of the visiting team with two out and the home team at bat. A man gets on base. Then another. Then the bases are loaded. The fourth batter hits a home run, and the home team wins 3–4. It ain't over till it's *over.*

Or take Wimbledon tennis. When the score is 40–love the sports announcer says, "Three championship points." Whoops. 40–30. "Two championship points." Then deuce. Oh dear. "One championship point," and then the championship is totally forfeited! It ain't over till it's *over.*

Over. There are at least thirty definitions of *over.* It could mean, "a position above," or "higher than." It could refer to "over" in the English sport cricket—"a set of six balls bowled from one end of a cricket match." It might refer to a pot of water boiling over. *Over* in this book means *done. Finished. Doomed. Dead in the water. No chance of changing, reversing, or being revived. No hope left. Caput* (from German *kaputt*—utterly defeated, hopelessly unable to function). In other words, when it is totally, utterly, and irrevocably *over.*

There are several ways "it ain't over till it's over" may be applied. One way is not wanting things to be over; you want things to continue—at least until there is a happy ending. Another way could refer to a sense of relief—when you are glad it's *over.* However, this book is mostly about not giving up—or jumping to conclusions—until there is a satisfying closure or a happy ending.

PART I

GOD'S WAYS

CHAPTER 1

NEVER TOO LATE,
NEVER TOO EARLY

*How long, O LORD? Will you forget me forever? How long will
you hide your face from me? How long must I wrestle with
my thoughts and day after day have sorrow in my heart?*
—PSALM 13:1–2

*"Wait on the Lord" is a constant refrain in the Psalms, and
it is a necessary word, for God often keeps us waiting. He
is not in such a hurry as we are, and it is not His way
to give more light on the future than we need for action
for the present, or to guide us more than one step at a
time. When in doubt, do nothing, but continue to wait
on God. When action is needed, light will come.[1]*
—J. I. PACKER

I REMEMBER WHERE I was on August 28, 1963—the day Martin Luther King delivered his, "I Have a Dream," speech. I saw it live on television, feeling the boldness and passion of his dream that "in Alabama little black boys and black girls will be able to join hands with little white boys and white girls as sisters and brothers."[2] Nothing seemed more impossible or far-fetched at the time. But not now.

I too have a dream. It may seem even more far-fetched, that the Word and the Spirit will come together in the church as in the Book of Acts. If you have followed my ministry, you will know that I maintain that there has been a silent divorce in the church between the Word and the Spirit. Speaking generally, those on the Word side emphasize the historic gospel and sound teaching such as justification by faith alone and the sovereignty of God. Those on the Spirit side emphasize signs, wonders, miracles, and all the gifts of the Spirit in operation as in the earliest church.

I'm sorry, but—with few exceptions—there is little sign of my dream being fulfilled at the moment. But "it ain't over till it's over." I happen to believe it is coming. Soon.

Are you tired of waiting on God? Have you been saying, "I've waited long enough"? Waiting on God to act can truly be one of the most difficult things we ever have to do.

And yet not waiting on Him can turn out to be one of the worst things we have ever done. Not waiting on Him often leads to great regret and sometimes despair.

One of the most exasperating ways of God is His *slowness* to step in on our behalf. But the more we get to know Him, the more we see that His slowness is not such a bad thing after all; it is for our good.

What if you could ask for anything you honestly want?

Have you ever fantasized that God might come to you as He did to Moses, and ask you what you want Him to do for you? What if He did come to you and invited you to ask for anything you like? What do you suppose you would ask for? And what if there were no conditions—that is, you need not ask for what is noble, altruistic, or even God honoring—that it could even be a selfish request? You simply have an opportunity to ask for *one thing* and it will be answered. What would you request?

God had let Moses know He was pleased with him: "You have found favor with me," the Lord said to him. Moses seized the moment and replied to God, "If you are pleased with me, *teach me your ways* so I may know you" (Exod. 33:13, emphasis added).

One of the things Moses learned about God's ways is His slowness to act.

The example of Moses's request to know God's ways suggests to me:

1. The kind of prayer a truly godly person could ask of God when given the chance.

2. That God answers our prayers when He is pleased with our requests.

We will see in this book that God *hears* us when we ask according to His will (1 John 5:14). When God *hears* us it means He will obey our requests. The Hebrew word *shamar* means "to hear so as to obey." God heard Moses's request.

Moses was arguably the greatest leader of men in human

history. He might have asked for any number of things—vengeance on His enemies, for example. But the truth of his heart surfaced: Moses wanted to know God's *ways*. This convicts me. I ask: Would I want to know God's *ways* above any other request?

I will admit to you that Moses's request puts me to shame. I cannot remember asking that of God. I certainly asked for a lot of other things.

I want to finish well. I would have thought that the safest guarantee that one will finish well is to make Moses's request—*to know God's ways*—your true desire.

The apostle Paul's supreme wish was the same—"that I may know Him," that is, Jesus Christ (Phil. 3:10, NKJV). You may want to ask, "Paul, are you saying that you don't know the Lord?" Of course Paul knew the Lord. But his deepest longing was to know Christ better. That is what he meant by the words, "That I may know him."

I have learned this. The better you get to know God the more you want to know Him. The more you know Him the more you are in awe of Him. The more you know Him, the more you want to spend time with Him. The more time you spend with Him, the more you feel you need Him. The best way to get to know anybody is to spend time with them. And so too when it comes to knowing God.

Moses frequented what was called the tent of meeting. It was there that the Lord spoke to Moses "face to face, just as a man speaks to his friend" (Exod. 33:11, MEV). It was in the tent of meeting that Moses put his request to the Lord—that he might know God's *ways*.

God lamented that ancient Israel did not know His ways (Heb. 3:10). God wants us to know His ways. But we must be prepared for this: His ways are different from our ways. What if we don't like God's ways?

> "For my thoughts are not your thoughts, neither are your ways my ways," declares the LORD. "As the heavens are higher than the earth, so are my ways higher than your ways and my thoughts than your thoughts."
> —ISAIAH 55:8–9

One of God's ways is His slowness. "With the Lord a day is like a thousand years, and a thousand years are like a day" (2 Pet. 3:8). Time is His domain. He is in no hurry. But we are. God can—to us—seem *so slow.*

SOMETIMES GOD ACTS QUICKLY

And yet God can act so quickly when He chooses. When Hezekiah took the lead in bringing about the purifying of the ancient temple, so long overdue, "all the people rejoiced at what God had brought about for his people, because *it was done so quickly*" (2 Chron. 29:36, emphasis added). God waited thousands of years before the Word was made flesh. "But when the set time had fully come, God sent his Son, born of a woman, born under the law, to redeem those under the law, that we might receive adoption to sonship" (Gal. 4:4–5). So once Jesus was born, "*Suddenly* a great company of the heavenly host appeared with the angel, praising God and saying, 'Glory to God in the highest heaven, and on earth peace to those on whom his favor rests'" (Luke 2:13–14, emphasis added). The church waited for hundreds of years for Joel's prophecy of the Holy Spirit to come. Finally "when the day of Pentecost came...*suddenly* a sound like the blowing of a violent wind came from heaven and filled the whole house where they were sitting" (Acts 2:1–2, emphasis added).

God promised Abraham a son when he was eighty-five and his wife, Sarah, was seventy-five. It was an extraordinary thing that God would declare such a promise when these two were so old! Why ever did God wait until then? That was when God told Abraham to "count the stars…so shall your offspring be," Abraham might have said, "Nonsense. Do you expect me at my age to believe that?" But Abraham *did* believe it! What is more, his faith was counted as righteousness (Gen. 15:6). This moment became Paul's exhibit A for his teaching of justification by faith alone (Rom. 4).

But after a few years it seemed that Abraham believed for nothing. No son was born. At Sarah's suggestion, Abraham slept with her handmaid, Hagar, in an effort to make things happen—to make good God's promise to him. All that was needed, they reasoned, was that the baby be male. Ishmael was born. Abraham assumed this was what God meant from the start. For the next thirteen years Abraham fully believed that Ishmael was the promised son. But Abraham was wrong. God informed Abraham after all those years that Sarah herself would conceive. She did. Isaac was born.

Why did Abraham have to wait so long? Why did not God tell Abraham from the start that Sarah would conceive? Why wait until he was nearly one hundred and she was ninety?

One of God's ways is His slowness. Moses was born when the people of Israel were undergoing extreme suffering. All of the Hebrew male babies were being killed by Pharaoh. Moses however was wonderfully preserved and grew up in the palace of Pharaoh. Forty years later Moses decided to reveal himself as an Israelite. Those forty years certainly seemed long enough for the Israelites to suffer. But when Moses killed an Egyptian to prove his loyalty, his plans backfired. He had to wait *another forty* years before God began to use him.

Moses was eighty when God truly began to use him. Even then things moved slowly. God could have given Moses power to overcome Pharaoh the first day he went in to demand, "Let my people go" (Exod. 5:1). But Pharaoh's heart was hardened. He would not acquiesce; he even put more suffering than ever on the Israelites. Moses said to the Lord, "Why have you brought trouble on this people? Is this why you sent me? Ever since I went to Pharaoh to speak in your name, he has brought trouble on this people, and you have not rescued your people at all" (Exod. 5:22–23).

That is not all. God sent many plagues on Egypt, and Pharaoh still would not give in. It was not until the tenth plague—when the Passover was finally introduced and all the firstborn in Egypt were destroyed—that Pharaoh finally let the people go. There was still more. Another battle with Pharaoh came about before the children of Israel crossed the Red Sea.

The slowness of God is one of His ways.

IS THERE A REASON GOD IS SLOW?

So why is God slow in making things happen? He tells us why. We may or may not like the reason: *that He might gain greater glory.* The answer came as the children of Israel were about to cross the Red Sea. "I will harden the hearts of the Egyptians so that they will go in after them. And *I will gain glory* through Pharaoh and all his army, through his chariots and his horsemen.

The Egyptians will know that I am the Lord *when I gain glory through Pharaoh*" (Exod. 14:17–18, emphasis added).

So there it is: the reason for God's slowness. It's not about us. It's about Him. His glory is at the bottom of it all. God said to Pharaoh, "I raised you up for this very purpose, that I might display my power in you and that my name might be proclaimed in all the earth" (Rom. 9:17).

Probably the most offensive thing about God is His glory. I have heard it said again and again from various people, including theologians: "I don't want a God who needs glory and has to have glory and needs people to give Him glory." The thing is, this kind of reasoning sets well with the world. Does it surprise you?

> The person without the Spirit does not accept the things that come from the Spirit of God but considers them foolishness, and cannot understand them because they are discerned only through the Spirit.
> —1 Corinthians 2:14

The person who does not have the Holy Spirit assumes that his or her own mind is the supreme court of appeal when it comes to knowing what is true. The heart of the problem is the problem of the human heart; we think we are qualified to judge what is valid, good, and worthy of consideration.

There are two words for *glory*. The Hebrew is *kabodh*, which means "heaviness, weightiness." We may speak of someone, "throwing their weight around"—that's the idea. The Greek word is *doxa*—"glory, honor." *Doxa* comes from a root word that means "opinion." The glory of God is His opinion, His will. God "works out everything in conformity with the purpose of his will" (Eph. 1:11).

When we remember that His ways are higher than our ways, and His thoughts are higher than our thoughts, there is but one thing for us to do—if we are going to think clearly: accept God for the way He is, lower our voices, and not object to His ways.

The slowness of God is connected to His glory.

All of us are tempted to complain and grumble while we wait for so long for God to act. The suffering seems so unfair. God could stop it any time He chose to do so. But Jesus put it like this: "You will grieve, but your grief will turn to joy. A woman giving birth to a child has pain because her time has come; but when her baby is born in time she forgets the anguish because of her joy that a child is born into the world" (John 16:20–21).

That is the way our Lord Jesus assesses the suffering He allows us to go through. Whatever He puts us through—or allows us to go through—however long and hard, we will have no complaints in the end.

WHY DOES GOD ALLOW EVIL?

Habakkuk the prophet wanted to know why God allows evil. Fair question. I deal with this issue in more detail in my book *Totally Forgiving God*.[2] Wouldn't we all like to know the answer to this? God made a deal with Habakkuk—to *wait* for the answer. The answer will come. It awaits an appointed time. "It speaks of *the end* and will not prove false. Though it linger, wait for it; it will certainly come and will not delay" (Hab. 2:3). The end? Whatever does God mean by "the end"? The answer is: *the end*. The last day. As I try to show in *Totally Forgiving God*, then, and not before, God will clear His name and explain why He has allowed evil and suffering for thousands of years.

"Wait," God says to us. Wait. Those who are willing to clear God's name in advance of *the end* are declared "righteous"—just as Abraham was. Abraham was declared righteous by believing what God said. So too with the word to Habakkuk. Those who live by the *faithfulness of God* are declared righteous (Hab. 2:4)—a promise quoted three times in the New Testament (Rom. 1:17; Gal. 3:11; Heb. 10:38).

The God of the Bible is a God of glory (Acts 7:1–2). Whatever He does, it is for His glory. The longer He waits, the greater the glory. The greater the suffering for us, the greater the glory for Him. But it also means greater the reward and greater the joy for us.

The way God will clear His name is worth waiting for. It ain't over till it's over. When He clears His name, it's over. Finished. Done. Every mouth will be stopped.

All people will clear God's name in the end. "Every knee should bow…and every tongue acknowledge that Jesus Christ is Lord, to the glory of God the Father" (Phil. 2:10–11). Yes, every single person will do it; the saved and lost will do it. Not because the unsaved will delight to do so but because they will be convinced that they were wrong and God is blameless.

It is those who live by God's faithfulness who clear His name now. We are so privileged to do so because we have come to know His ways. Those who get to know His ways accept that He is a wise, wonderful, gracious God.

But is He not slow? Oh yes, to us. And God understands how we feel. He knows our frame and remembers that we are dust (Ps. 103:14). But one day our grief will be turned to joy.

And as for my own dream—that the Word and the Spirit will come together—I have observed all my life that God is *never too late, never too early, but always just on time.* The simultaneous combination of the Word and the Spirit in great measure will result in spontaneous combustion so that the church—and the world—will never be the same again.

And when that day comes, it will come suddenly.

CHAPTER 2

WHEN GOD PLAYS
HARD TO GET

If I were hungry I would not tell you, for the
world is mine, and all that is in it.
—PSALM 50:12

Patience is a fruit of the Spirit that grows only under trial. It
is useless to pray for patience. Well, actually I encourage you
to pray for patience, but I'll tell you what you'll get TRIALS![1]
—JOYCE MEYER

A DISTRAUGHT YOUNG WOMAN came into the vestry at
Westminster Chapel to get my advice. Her boyfriend
was suddenly distancing himself from her. It was because she
had been in his face day and night. He was now going on a trip

to a foreign country, and she could not bear having him away. She would phone him every night, but he would not return her calls. She said it was driving her crazy. It was easy to see that he was getting annoyed with her; she was devaluing herself in his eyes by chasing him. I said to her, "Mildred [not her real name], do you want to win Larry?"

"Oh yes please, I'm desperate," she said.

"Then stop phoning him. Quit bothering him. Keep out of his life entirely. Play hard to get." She said she could not do that; she needed to hear his voice every day. The anxiety was killing her. I told her that she was going to drive him completely away, that she must stop phoning him altogether and that, should he phone her, for her to be utterly unavailable to him. She confessed that she was incapable of this. I warned her that she would lose him entirely unless she started playing hard to get immediately.

Mildred finally took my advice. She said later that it was the hardest thing she ever had to do in her entire life. But she did it. She stopped phoning him. And when he eventually phoned her, she would not return his calls. She walked out of his life. But three months later he asked her to marry him, and I performed the wedding shortly after that.

Playing hard to get is to pretend to be less interested in someone or something than you really are as a way of making people more interested in you.

Politicians do it. The best way to become elected to office is—at first—to act as though you are not the slightest bit interested. Create a mystique. Make them chase you. Likewise, shrewd people applying for a job must sometimes play hard to get. If you show too much interest, you could devalue yourself. Preachers hoping to be called to a church often play hard to get. A pulpit committee is suspicious of a man who sends out résumés in order to get a better church.

GOD IS AMAZING!

But would God do that? Yes, sometimes. John Newton wrote about *amazing grace*. This chapter is about an amazing God! Think about the fact that our sovereign, majestic, omnipotent Creator and Redeemer—who made the universe and has billions of angels worshipping Him—would reach down to us. This is why the psalmist David asked, "What is man that You are mindful of him?" (Ps. 8:4, MEV). That is not all. Sometimes God becomes utterly vulnerable to criticism—momentarily acting as though He doesn't care. To do this He will sometimes disguise who He is and what He is up to in order to see how much we want Him. It is a different way of getting our attention. Extraordinary!

You might say, "Surely the great God of the universe would not lower Himself like that. Surely when people see His wrath and majesty and justice, they will come crawling to Him, begging for mercy." Quite right. That is the way it often happens. But believe it or not, sometimes it is the other way around; God graciously and humbly—strange as it may seem—acts as if He doesn't care in order to get our attention.

Sometimes a new prayer is answered the first day. But sometimes I put a request to God every day for a year and still get no answer. When God answers my prayer the first day He is certainly *not* playing *hard to get*.

God may have been playing hard to get for ten days right after Jesus ascended to heaven. Jesus told His followers *not to leave Jerusalem.* They were to wait for the Holy Spirit to fall on them. The one hundred twenty people who tarried had no idea how long they would have to wait on God. Those ten days may have seemed a long time. Not much was happening. But once the Spirit came, it would seem God stopped playing hard to get for a while. In the earliest church, as described in the Book of Acts, they seemed to get their prayers answered quickly; miracles were common, healings were common, answered prayer was common. God did not seem to play hard to get in those days. But in succeeding generations God seemed to withdraw His manifestations—with some exceptions—to a considerable degree. People had to wait for Him. Councils would deliberate as to the nature of the Son of God. What books should be included in the canon of Scripture? Things did not come easily as they appeared to do in the Book of Acts. For some reason God began playing hard to get.

So when I have to go back to the Lord day after day, year after year, whether to see a miracle or any prayer answered, it is probably because He is playing hard to get. This is one of His ways.

The thing is, when I bring a new request to Him, I have no idea how long I might have to keep praying. So what do I do? The answer is, I don't give up until it's over! It's not over until it's over. I know one thing for sure: snapping my finger at the Most High God and expecting Him to leap in my direction isn't going to work. I go to Him on bended knee.

SOMETIMES GOD SEEMS ALMOST PLAYFUL

In some books I have spoken of the "divine tease"—when God seems to be almost playful, even teasing us in the way He shows up. For example, when the disciples were in the boat in the storm on the Sea of Galilee, Jesus came to them but made out as if, without caring, He was going to go right past them! They thought

He was a ghost. They cried out because they all saw Him and were terrified. He then said, "Take courage! It is I! Don't be afraid" (Mark 6:50). He then demonstrated how much He cared, but not until they cried out.

The resurrected Christ walked alongside the two men on the road to Emmaus. But they were somehow kept from knowing it was Jesus. Coming to a village, "Jesus continued on as if he were going farther." But the two men "urged him strongly" to stay around (Luke 24:28–29). And that is exactly what Jesus wanted them to do! He wanted to see if merely from hearing His exposition of the Scriptures they would keep a stranger around who could expound the Word like that! The truth is that their hearts burned so deeply that they pleaded for Him to stay, not knowing—at first—that it was Jesus. That is exactly the result Jesus wanted of them.

This goes to show that anything that causes our hearts to burn when hearing the Word of God taught is a huge hint we should seize the moment. Times like these don't come around every day, but when they do we should make God's presence a priority over any other business at hand. "Seek the LORD while he may be found" (Isa. 55:6).

A Greek lady—born in Syrian Phoenicia—begged Jesus to drive the demon out of her daughter. Jesus appeared rude to her. "It is not right to take the children's bread and toss it to the dogs." Why did Jesus talk to her like that? He wanted to see how earnest she was. "Lord," she replied, "even the dogs under the table eat the children's crumbs." Jesus was pleased with the way the lady took this. "For such a reply, you may go; the demon has left your daughter." She went home and found her child lying on the bed, and the demon gone (Mark 7:24–30).

Why Does God
Play Hard to Get?

God plays hard to get with us to reveal our hearts. One evening when Jacob was alone, a man appeared from out of the blue and began wrestling with him. Having no idea who this man was or what it meant, Jacob wrestled with him till daybreak. When this stranger—who turned out to be an angel playing hard to get—saw that he could not overpower Jacob, he touched the socket of Jacob's hip so that his hip was wrenched as they wrestled. The angel said, "Let me go, for it is daybreak" (Gen. 32:26). At some point in this wrestling match Jacob realized that whoever it was that had leaped on him in the middle of the night was in fact the best thing that ever happened to him! Jacob was not going to let him out of his sight. He said, "I will not let you go unless you bless me" (vs. 26). This is when Jacob's name became Israel (Gen. 32:28). It was pivotal in his life. Martin Luther said that we must know God as an enemy before we can know Him as a friend. By this Luther meant that many people *feel* that God seems like an enemy—at first.

God put a proposition to Moses. He told Moses in so many words, "That's a sorry lot of people you are having to lead. They are not listening to you, they are not listening to Me. I'll tell you what, Moses, I am going to destroy this nation. Then you and I can start out with an entirely new nation that will be stronger than these rebellious people—how about that, Moses?" (Num. 14:11–12, author paraphrase).

Many of us might have said, "Yes! Let's do that."

God wanted to reveal Moses's heart. Would Moses take the offer? Or would he intercede for these people? The answer is: Moses interceded for them. He replied to God in so many words, "Lord, You must not do that. Your great name is at stake. What will they say about Your great name back in Egypt? They will say that the Lord was not able to bring these people to the land He promised them on oath" (Num. 14:13–16, author paraphrase).

Moses's response was the very response God wanted. The psalmist later wrote that God said He would destroy the people of Israel "had not Moses, his chosen one, stood in the breach before him to keep his wrath from destroying them" (Ps. 106:23).

Sometimes the Lord puts obstacles in our way to see what we truly want in our heart of hearts. The divine tease to Moses worked. It showed what kind of man he was. Moses could have said, "Yes Lord, destroy these people. I've had enough." But no. He prayed for them.

If God answered our prayers every single time we prayed, we might devalue prayer—and Him. Whether you call it the divine tease or God playing hard to get, it is for our good.

WHEN GOD HIDES HIS FACE

So too when God hides His face. "Truly you are a God who has been hiding himself, the God and Savior of Israel," so Isaiah discovered (Isa. 45:15). All of God's children sooner or later find this out about God—whether or not they were taught it in advance—God will hide His face. This is a metaphor to indicate when God's presence is not as real as it was, when He is not answering prayer as He had been doing, when He is not helping us to understand His Word as He previously did.

One of the reasons God hides His face and plays hard to get is to slow down any tendency we might have to take ourselves too seriously. This frankly is one of my greatest weaknesses—to take myself too seriously. The people who take themselves too seriously are those who must always be right—or think they are—and become almost obsessive with being seen as right. It is a consequence of being self-centered. We also become insensitive to others. People like us need to learn to laugh at ourselves, to loosen up a bit.

When God hides His face from us, it has the effect of showing us how devoid of wisdom we are when left to ourselves. I'm afraid I need it all the time. It can be embarrassing, especially if we are prone to the *Elijah complex*—that I and I alone am left. God had to teach Elijah a lesson (1 Kings 19:10). God can hide Himself—then show up again. This scenario can be effective in slowing us down and can make us smell the roses and not be so uptight.

Another danger for some of us is to develop an overfamiliarity with God—and a feeling of entitlement. He becomes a *buddy*, a *pal*. This is not good; it is unhealthy and might even cheapen the God of the Bible. Whereas He does indeed stoop to our level, making Himself appear vulnerable, it is not God's design that we forget who He is. A likely consequence of an overfamiliarity with God, then, is that this feeling of entitlement creeps in. If we are not careful, we might begin to think God owes us something, that we are entitled to demand things from Him.

Caution: do not go there. One of the curses of our age is a feeling of entitlement that people have.

These tendencies therefore show some of the reasons God hides His face from us and why He plays hard to get: lest we become impertinent in His presence. This is why we are told to "seek" His face. Why seek His face? Because He hides His face. He plays hard to get.

> When You said, "Seek My face," my heart said to you, "Your face, LORD, I will seek." Do not hide Your face far from me.
> —PSALM 27:8–9, MEV

The essence of most trials is God hiding His face. Mind you, that trial could be financial reverse. Losing your keys when you are rushing to leave your home. Physical setbacks. Having a friend misunderstand you. Your putting your foot in it and you know someone is offended. When a relationship has turned sour. When vindication is postponed. Someone offended you and you lose your temper. Sleeplessness. You showed no wisdom in a major decision. You were late for a critically important appointment. You lost your job. You failed an exam. You were rejected for a position that had been promised to you.

"Why, Lord?" We all ask this. At the bottom God seems ten thousand miles away. Is He playing hard to get? Yes. It is His way of saying, "Seek My face."

You seek because you have not found what you wanted. The word *seek* means "attempt to find." You look for what has been missing. You make an effort. So with seeking God's face. It is when He is playing hard to get in order to find out how serious you are in wanting a right relationship with Him. You cannot command it—that is when you have let entitlement kick in. Rather, you ask for it. "Ask and it will be given to you; seek and you will find" (Matt. 7:7).

Would God Actually Yearn for My Company?

A number of years ago I came across Psalm 50:12: "If I were hungry I would not tell you." For some reason I could not shake off a deep, deep feeling that God *was* trying to speak to me. Why ever would He say, "If I were hungry I would not tell you"? It came to me: "He's telling me precisely that—right now. He wants my attention. He is whispering to me that He is longing for me to spend time with Him." Is He hungry? For me? I was so gripped that I spent the next day praying and fasting. Why ever would God keep it to Himself if He were hungry? Why bother to tell me that He would not tell me— unless He *was* making Himself vulnerable by telling me right then: "I want time with you."

God cannot demonstrate His love more to me than when He plays hard to get with me. It shows He cares.

To put it another way, when He does not show up after a few days I might say, "I don't think God cares or He would not distance Himself from me like that." Or I might say, "What if He is sending a signal to me—I am wanting your company today?"

If you ask, "What do you mean by His not showing up after a few days?" I answer: it is when He does not manifest Himself— as when I get holy nudges from the Holy Spirit. Or if I don't see something fresh when I read His word. Or—when preaching—I don't see people come to the Lord. When I preach the Gospel, I expect to see people converted. When I pray, I expect to sense God's presence. When I read the Bible, I expect that the Word will unfold itself with ease. So when these things don't happen, I ask myself: "What is God up to?"

When we know more of His *ways*, we may well discern what the Lord is saying to us.

Myriad are the ways of God. The list is endless. And if we are able to discern that God is allowing a trial in order not only to teach us patience but also to reveal our hearts, we may take comfort. It means He hasn't finished with us yet.

CHAPTER 3

THE MYSTERY OF PRAYER

You do not have, because you do not ask God. When
you ask, you do not receive, because you ask with wrong
motives, that you may spend what you get on pleasures.
—JAMES 4:2–3

What we say in prayer actually moves
the Lord to change things.[1]
—JONI EARECKSON TADA

T HE GREATEST FRINGE benefit of being a Christian is the
privilege of prayer. The *main* benefit of being a Christian,
as we will see in chapter 11, is to know you will go to heaven
when you die. And yet God throws in other benefits—getting to
know Him by reading the Bible, the assurance of His guidance,

and the knowledge He has a plan for our lives. But—in my opinion—the greatest privilege of all is that of prayer.

Questions You Might Have Been Afraid to Ask

And yet prayer is a huge mystery. We will see that it is closely connected to the greatest question of all—the problem of evil and suffering. Why does God tell us to pray? Why would He tell us to pray if He could do what we ask without our asking? Does He ask us to pray regarding what He has already decided to do? And why, having asked us to pray, does He not answer us when we pray? Why does prayer sometimes work?

Does prayer really influence God? Does He wait to act until we pray? What motivates us to pray—or *who* motivates us to pray? Is it God who is behind our praying when we have a burden that drives us to prayer? If so, why is it that praying with a burden does not always get results?

Why does God often step in—whether we pray or not?

Do some people have more influence with God than others? Would I be better off if I asked Elijah or Paul to pray for me than to ask you?

Does the number of people praying about a particular matter influence God? So do thousands praying have more influence in heaven than one person? Does God side with 51 percent of people who ask rather than the 49 percent who also pray but ask for a different outcome? Does God want us to lobby for issues by recruiting others to pray about a specific issue? If so, who does He listen to? Does He count how many people pray for a certain matter before He decides to answer?

Why would the great apostle Paul request prayer from ordinary Christians?

Why did Jesus pray?

These are just a few of the questions one can raise when it comes to the subject of prayer. In a word: prayer is a deep mystery.

Did you ever notice that there is no "gift" of praying in the New Testament? Look at the gifts of the Holy Spirit in 1 Corinthians 12:8–10, 28–31, or the motivational gifts in Romans 12:3–8. There is no gift of prayer listed. Furthermore, none of the fruit of the Spirit in Galatians 5:22–23 includes prayer.

There are more than two hundred specific references to prayer in the New Testament, taken largely from two Greek words for prayer: *proseuche* and *deesis*; they can be used interchangeably. My book *Did You Think to Pray?* was written mainly to motivate Christians—and church leaders—to spend more *time* in prayer.[2] The average church leader in America and Britain spends between four and five minutes a day in prayer—a far cry from the prayer lives of many of the great men and women of God in church history who often spent two hours a day in private personal prayer. This to me partly explains the powerlessness of many leaders today.

NO PRAYING WHEN WE GET TO HEAVEN

So many mysteries will be unfolded and made clear to us when we get to heaven. We shall understand prayer better there than we do now, except that there will be no praying when we get to heaven! One of the most intriguing lines in the hymn "Sweet Hour of Prayer," written by a blind preacher, comes right at the end in this final verse:

Sweet hour of prayer! Sweet hour of prayer!
May I thy consolation share,
Till, from Mount Pisgah's lofty height,
I view my home and take my flight.
This robe of flesh I'll drop, and rise
To seize the everlasting prize,
And shout, while passing through the air,
"Farewell, farewell, sweet hour of prayer!"[3]
—William Walford (1772–1850)

There will be no praying in heaven. Prayer is our most wonderful privilege on our way to heaven.

It will be so exciting to learn in heaven what went on when our prayers ascended to the throne of grace. In the Book of Revelation we get brief, if not tantalizing, glimpses of heaven. It is apparently a noisy place. Filled with color. Worship and praise continues nonstop with God's creation shouting:

Holy, holy, holy is the Lord God Almighty, who was, and is, and is to come.
—Revelation 4:8

How amidst this praise does God also take time to listen to each prayer of His people—one at a time—as if there were no one else praying? St. Augustine said that God loves every person as if there were no one else to love; so too does God listen to every one of us as though there were no one else talking to Him. I know that one of the angels had a golden censer. He stood at the altar.

He was given much incense to offer, with the prayers of all God's people, on the golden altar in front of the throne.

28

The smoke of the incense, together with the prayers of
God's people, went up before God from the angel's hand.
—REVELATION 8:3–4

Does this mean there is an angel whose role in heaven is to
look after the prayers of the saints? Are these prayers bottled up,
so to speak, waiting for a time they will be answered?

I don't know. The references to the "prayers of the saints" tell
me that our prayers are taken seriously in heaven. None of them
goes unnoticed. God knows every single one of them and who
prayed each one and when they were first uttered on the earth.

There is so much about prayer I do not understand. It is an
unfathomable mystery.

SEVEN THINGS I KNOW
FOR SURE ABOUT PRAYER

Although I am not claiming to understand them, there are some
things that I do know for sure about prayer.

1. Jesus told us to pray and not give up.

The greatest encouragement to pray and keep on praying is
when Jesus gave a parable to show why people should never give
up asking for the same old thing. "Jesus told his disciples a parable to show them that they should always pray and not give up"
(Luke 18:1). There follows the Parable of the Persistent Widow.
Her request, if anything, was a bit selfish: "Grant me justice
against my adversary" (v. 3). This shows that we do not necessarily have to put *pious* requests to God; we may ask what is on
our hearts. This widow went to an uncaring, insensitive judge
daily with the same old request. But the judge finally gave into
her request. The point of the parable is, how much more will

our loving heavenly Father come to our aid when we cry out to Him day and night? We should therefore never give up praying.

2. Prayer makes a huge difference in the way I feel.

While this may be entirely subjective, I can only say that the more I pray, the better I feel; the earlier in the day I pray, the better I feel. It could be the presence of the Holy Spirit; sometimes it is, sometimes perhaps it is not. It could be entirely psychological that I feel better when I go through my prayer list—item by item, day after day. I don't know. I certainly do know I feel better when I do; I feel worse when I don't. So I keep it up.

3. Prayer can be work and not fun.

Who said it would be fun in any case? That said, a friend of mine—Jeremy Jennings, who has been on the staff at London's Holy Trinity Brompton for years—has a gift of making corporate prayer fun. He can make a one-hour prayer meeting seem like five minutes. But what if there is no Jeremy Jennings around to lead prayer meetings? And what do you do when you are alone? Paul said we must be ready "in season and out of season" (2 Tim. 4:2), a phrase I have always taken to refer partly to praying. Sometimes you feel like praying, sometimes you don't. Don't wait for the Spirit to *move* you. Pray anyway, daily, whether you feel like it or not. The truth is, it is more work than fun.

4. God answers some of my prayers, but not all of them.

Does this surprise you? Why some and not all? First, it could be because some of the things I ask for are not in God's will. They may seem reasonable to me. But they may not be what God wants for me. Second, "it ain't over till it's over"; sometimes a prayer not being answered could be only what *appears* to be unanswered. God may decide to answer my prayer tomorrow. For that reason I don't give up praying; I want to be found ready should He answer that request I may have long since dismissed as out of the question.

5. Those whom God used the most were almost always people who prayed a lot.

This is huge for me. If I am totally honest, this is almost certainly one of the main reasons I have endeavored to have a strong, consistent prayer life for the last sixty years. I tried to pray two hours a day—quiet time, not sermon preparation time—when I was at Westminster Chapel. I still do the same thing now that I am *retired* and on the road and writing books. Until I learn otherwise I choose to believe my best days lie ahead. And when I face the sobering reality that my best days are past—which I will, I would hope to keep up praying as much as I ever did. For God has been so good to me.

6. God answers prayers when they are according to His will.

Like it or not, that is the way it is, as we will see further below. But I can live with that. God only wants what is best for us. When we don't get what we want, it may seem like a deprivation or disappointment, but we will inevitably come to see that His idea for us is what is best. When I think of the principle that God only answers prayers He is happy with, I cannot forget this ominous word: "So he gave them what they asked for, but sent a wasting disease among them" (Ps. 106:15). The most foolish thing I can do, then, is to persist in asking for what is not right. I will know it is not right when it clearly and unmistakably goes against God's will—as when the children of Israel tried too late to enter Canaan (Num. 14:41–45), or when they demanded a king against God's will (1 Sam. 8:4–22).

7. Satan does not want us to pray.

This may be the greatest motivation of all to pray! Archbishop William Temple is famous for his comment, "When I pray, coincidences happen, and when I don't pray, they don't."[4] And yet one of the most gripping comments I have ever read regarding prayer is by Paul Billheimer, who reckons that Satan does not care how much people read about prayer "if only he can keep them from praying."[4] It is enough for me to know that Satan does not want us to pray. One of the best ways to know the will of God is to figure out what you imagine the devil would want you to do, then do the opposite. I therefore reckon that when I pray it is at least one time I know I am doing something right.

> Satan trembles, when he sees the weakest saint upon his knees.[6]
> —WILLIAM COWPER

One further compelling reason to spend time in prayer was put by Sister Theresa (not Mother Teresa) to my friend J. John when he was in India: "God likes your company." And that, just maybe, is one of the main reasons God does not always answer our prayers—at first; He wants our attention. He likes our company. Were He to answer all our prayers quickly we might not spend as much time with Him.

Yes, prayer is a mystery. But one thing is for sure: if we wait until we understand prayer, we will never pray. So I urge us to get on with it and not wait until we figure it out.

CHAPTER 4

UNANSWERED PRAYER

*Father, if you are willing, take this cup from
me; yet not my will, but yours be done.*
—LUKE 22:42

*I am profoundly grateful to God that He did not
grant me certain things for which I asked, and
that He shut certain doors in my face.*[1]
—D. MARTYN LLOYD-JONES (1899–1981)

I F I HAD to decide which has been the greater blessing to
me in my eighty years—whether answered prayer or unanswered prayer, I am absolutely *not sure* which has become more
precious to me. I have recently sought to recall how many
prayers of mine that were answered when I was young. I can

barely recall prayers that were answered during those days. But I can vividly remember prayers that were definitely *not* answered—especially those regarding my mother who fell critically ill at the age of forty-three when I was seventeen. And yet this reminds me of a lady, aged ninety, who had influence on my mother when my mother was a teenager. The old saint would say, "I have served the Lord for so long now that I can hardly tell the difference between a blessing and a trial."

During the time of my mother's illness I felt that God gave me a girlfriend to give me comfort—and especially after my mother passed away. I entered Trevecca Nazarene College (now University) in the autumn of 1953, where my new—and first—girlfriend had been a student. Indeed she was what I thought I needed in my grief. I was convinced she would be my wife one day. I certainly prayed for that. But in fact she jilted me.

Have you lived long enough to thank God for unanswered prayer? Can you recall that which you wanted so desperately but which was not granted?

In this chapter we will examine some examples of unanswered prayer and how unanswered prayer became beautifully strategic in the purpose of God for His people.

If you have followed my ministry over the years, you may recall that I used to sell vacuum cleaners door to door for a living. Before getting married I did not know how to handle money and got deep in debt. I bought an airplane, a new 1957 Edsel, an expensive stereo system, and other things. Perhaps Louise and I should have waited, but we didn't. Also I had not completed my university degree. I was, however, in the ministry in those early years of marriage—but only just. I was ordained and preached regularly in churches on Sundays in and around

Fort Lauderdale. I had a radio broadcast called *The Redeemer's Witness*, and I edited a monthly magazine called by that name. But in order to pay my debts I had to work hard in the secular world. I thought those days would never end. All the promises I thought God had given me regarding an international ministry one day seemed out of the question.

I was invited to be the associate pastor of First Baptist Church in Hallandale, Florida. Sometime later the pastor who invited me there moved to another church, and it was assumed I would be called to be the succeeding pastor. I was so pleased about this. With no university or seminary degree, I was very fortunate that I would be called to be the senior pastor of a substantial church. This seemed to be the answer to my prayers. I shared this exciting news with one of my old mentors, Dr. John Logan. He said to me, "There's many a slip between the cup and the lip." That gave me pause. Indeed, at the church meeting a few days later—in which I was to be routinely called to be the pastor, lo and behold, they rejected me. I was devastated. It was one of the great disappointments of my life.

I now look back on those days with the sweetest sense of relief and gratitude to God that the church in Hallandale wanted someone else. First, had I become the pastor there I would almost certainly never have aspired to finish my university degree or go to seminary. But I became the minister of the Lauderdale Manors Baptist Church in Fort Lauderdale soon afterward, and because of this I ended up getting my bachelor's degree and was accepted at Southern Baptist Theological Seminary in Louisville, Kentucky. This led to our move to England.

While at Westminster Chapel Louise and I had some of our vacations in America. During one summer we had arranged for us to meet an old girlfriend, who was, I thought—as did nearly everyone—the most gorgeous girl around. Had the Lord let me marry her it would have been an incredible answer to prayer. But it didn't happen. Never mind. Louise and I were now scheduled to see her. On the way to the restaurant I turned on the radio and a country-western song was being sung: "Thank God for Unanswered Prayer." It was written by a man who had been jilted by his childhood sweetheart. But when he saw her several years later he wrote this song. Having no idea this would be somewhat prophetic for me, I turned off the radio, and we went into the restaurant to see my old friend. I will never forget it. I looked at her. Then I looked at Louise and thought, "Thank God for unanswered prayer."

GOD ONLY WANTS WHAT IS BEST FOR US

God only wants what is best for us. Hardly a week goes by in which I do not think of these words: "No good thing does he withhold from those whose walk is blameless" (Ps. 84:11). Thankfully that does not mean we must be sinlessly perfect—or no one would have the benefit of this verse. It refers to those whose bent of life is in the direction of pleasing God day and night. I think also of these words: "Delight yourself in the LORD, and He will give you the desires of your heart" (Ps. 37:4, MEV). Indeed, "He fulfills the desires of those who fear him" (Ps. 145:19).

Our Lord Jesus Christ at this moment is seated at the right hand of the Father. He is interceding for us. One of the things Jesus does, as John Calvin put it, speaking metaphorically, is to beckon for the attention of the Father to Himself "to keep His gaze away from our sins." But there is more that Jesus does. He prays for us according to the will of God as also the Holy Spirit prays for us according to the will of God (Rom. 8:26–27). We therefore have Jesus and the Holy Spirit simultaneously praying for us right now! Robert Murray M'Cheyne once said, "If I could hear Christ praying for me in the next room, I would not fear a million of enemies. Yet the distance makes no difference; He is praying for me."[2]

But there is more. In keeping the Father's gaze away from our sins, Jesus also filters our prayer requests. God only *hears* prayers that are in His will. As we saw above, the Hebrew word *shamar* means to hear in the sense that you obey. Of course God knows everything and hears everything. But if He obeys our request, it means He *hears* us in this Hebraic sense. For if we ask anything according to God's will, He hears us (1 John 5:14). So I reckon Jesus passes those requests to the Father that He knows will please Him. When you and I pray in Jesus's name, we address the Father. But fortunately for us, the Father does not obey all our requests! This is because Jesus only lets the Father hear those requests that are in the will of God.

WHY SOME OF OUR REQUESTS DON'T GET TO THE FATHER

To illustrate this principle, here is a story out of the Great Reformation. In those days there was considerable difference of opinion as to the true meaning of the Eucharist—the partaking of the bread and wine at the Lord's Table. The Roman Catholics maintained that the bread and wine literally became the body and blood of Jesus when the priest pronounced the words, "This is My body." This was called transubstantiation. Martin Luther had his view—called consubstantiation, although it was virtually the same as the Catholics. At the other extreme was the view of Huldrych Zwingli (1484–1531) who argued that the

Lord's Supper was but a *memorial* of the Last Supper, referring to the words, "This do in remembrance of me" (1 Cor. 11:25). John Calvin had an entirely different perspective. He said that the *spiritual* presence of Christ by faith was present in the sacraments. He wrote a letter to Martin Luther, outlining his point of view, certain that he could convince Luther. But the letter was intercepted by Philip Melanchthon, Luther's close friend and aide. Melanchthon believed that the letter would not please Luther. So Luther never knew that a letter had been sent by Calvin.

And yet that is what our Lord Jesus does at the Father's right hand. Some of our requests do not get through to the Father. "When you ask, you do not receive, because you ask with wrong motives, that you may spend what you get on your pleasures" (James 4:3). For our Lord Jesus knows the will of the Father and therefore intercedes only according to His will.

God says *no* to our prayer requests because He has a better idea than we do as to what is best for us. This is beautifully illustrated by Jesus's turning down a request for Him to come to Bethany to heal Lazarus. When Mary and Martha sent word to Jesus that His close friend, their brother, Lazarus, was seriously ill, they assumed Jesus would come immediately to Bethany to heal him. But Jesus did not go. He stayed where He was. His disciples were perplexed. Jesus then gave the reason for not going.

There Is a Reason God Does Not Answer Our Prayer

It is estimated that each year one million children are trafficked for slave labor or sexual exploitation.[3] Where is God when these people cry to Him?

Jesus's answer is one of the profoundest statements in the entire Bible. It not only explains part of the reason for unanswered prayer, but also gives a strong hint why God allows evil and suffering. *Why does God not step in and relieve suffering when He so easily could?* The answer is partly for the same reason Jesus did not stop what He was doing and go straight to Bethany to heal Lazarus—which He could have done. Knowing that His disciples did not understand, Jesus simply said, "Lazarus is dead." In other words, if Lazarus is dead, why bother? But then He added, "And for your sake I am glad I was not there [in Bethany], *so that you may believe*" (John 11:13–14, emphasis added).

There it is, one of the reasons God does not say *yes* to our prayer requests—or stop evil and suffering: *that we might have faith.* After all, if you knew the reason for evil, you would not need faith at all. Furthermore, if God instantly answered every single request you put to Him, you would not really need faith. But for some reason God has chosen to create a universe in which people must believe His Word. It is *faith* that pleases God (Heb. 11:6). Therefore God not telling us why He allows suffering is an opportunity for us to believe Him. To trust Him. Likewise, God not telling us the reason He does not answer our prayers is that we might trust Him.

Therefore God says *no* to some of our requests partly because He is looking for faith in us when we don't get what we want. It is also because God likes our company, as I put it in my book *Did You Think to Pray?* But there is another reason for unanswered prayer: He has a better idea than what we asked for.

Jesus did not tell the disciples what He had in mind. He knew that the Father's strategy all along was to raise Lazarus from the dead—surely a better idea than keeping him from dying! But Jesus did not tell the disciples that.

Nor does God always give us the reason He does not answer our prayers. He wants to see our reactions. He wants to see if we will love Him whether or not He does what pleases us.

When Jesus showed up in Bethany four days after Lazarus's funeral, both Martha and Mary were distressed. "If you had been here, my brother would not have died," each of them said (John 11:21, 32). Whereas this does indicate a measure of faith in Jesus, faith was not what Martha or Mary were wanting to convey. They implicitly blamed Jesus for not coming when He could have—to keep Lazarus from dying. Mary was especially weeping over Lazarus's death. Perhaps she was also feeling a bit bitter. Jesus did not scold her. He did not moralize her. "Jesus wept" (John 11:35), this being the shortest verse in the Bible. And yet He knew exactly what He was going to do in a few moments. But He still wept with Mary.

So too with us. Jesus knows what things will be like tomorrow and a week from now. But He realizes we don't know. So what does He do? Does He rebuke us? Make us feel guilty? No. He weeps with us. He lives with us in the here and now.

In this scenario of unanswered prayer the twelve disciples, as well as Mary and Martha, were getting an intimate glimpse into God's *ways*. God lamented that ancient Israel did not know His "ways" (Heb. 3:10). When Moses could have asked for anything under the sun, he asked to know God's "ways" (Exod. 33:13)—a great tribute to Moses's heart that he would ask for this.

Unanswered prayer is an opportunity to get to know God's ways. Unanswered prayer is a situation He allows in order to get our attention—when we don't get what we want. So what do we do? We continue to wait before Him.

You will recall that Abraham at the age of eighty-five was given the promise of a son. Because the fulfillment of the promise was delayed, Abraham slept with Sarah's mistress, Hagarm, to speed up the promise; Ishmael was born. As we saw, for the next thirteen years Abraham assumed that Ishmael was the promised son. But when he was told that Sarah would conceive after all this and that Isaac was coming, Abraham was not happy. He put a request to God that would be utterly unanswered: "If only Ishmael [rather than Isaac] might live under your blessing!" (Gen. 17:18). Abraham was grieved that Isaac, not Ishmael, was the promise God had in mind all along.

It was not easy for Abraham to accept God's plan. Those were extremely hard days for him. But Isaac was born, and Abraham submitted to the will of God. Abraham was called the friend of God—what an amazing position to be in! But God still displeased Abraham with His plan. We too may be known as God's friends, but sometimes we have to accept unhappy news. It was the future of God's covenant people generally that He had in mind by not answering Abraham's prayer. Abraham acquiesced for the sake of the future of the people of God.

UNANSWERED PRAYER IS NOT ALWAYS ABOUT US

Unanswered prayer may not pertain to us as much as it does to the secret will of God for His wider eternal strategies. Answered prayer therefore may be owing to a higher purpose of God that we could not possibly grasp at the time. When Rick Warren began his book *The Purpose- Driven Life* with the words, "It's not about you,"[4] it is because the purpose of God generally is more important than our own wants and wishes.

How would it make you feel if you knew that your unanswered prayer was not about you but rather about God's higher purpose for His glory? Could you live with that? Sometimes it *is* for you. I am glad I was rejected in Hallandale, Florida. I am glad God gave me Louise. But I may not know until I get to heaven how many of my prayers have gone unanswered because God was looking after His people down the road!

"There's a purpose in it," one of my oldest mentors, Billy Ball, used to say to me. When anything disappointing or upsetting occurred, Billy would always say, "There's a purpose in it."

Do you believe that? Can you live with that?

The greatest example of unanswered prayer, however, was in the Garden of Gethsemane. It is when Jesus was on the brink of the greatest trial and suffering that any person had ever—ever—experienced. Sweating drops of blood in the anticipated agony of the cross, Jesus asked the Father, if possible, to grant permission for Him to avoid the cross. "Father, if you are willing, take this cup from me; yet not my will, but yours be done" (Luke 22:42).

Has it ever crossed your mind what the world would have been had the Father answered Jesus's prayer? It is unthinkable. The possibility is too vast to contemplate.

THE FATHER DID NOT ANSWER JESUS'S PRAYER

In any case God did not answer Jesus's prayer. He went to the cross. He suffered injustice; all the accusations were false. He suffered physical pain; crucifixions are known to be most horrible kind of death ever conceived. He suffered embarrassment;

He was naked on the cross before all those who looked on. He suffered being misunderstood; His followers felt betrayed that Jesus would allow Himself to be crucified since He could have stopped it. He suffered the taunts of the crowds, knowing that if He replied in kind He would sin—and therefore not be the spotless, sinless Lamb of God. Worst of all, Jesus endured the unprecedented wrath of God Almighty. The only time Jesus did not address His Father as Father was when He cried out, "My God, my God, why have you forsaken me?" (Matt. 27:46). This was the moment when the Lord laid on Jesus the iniquity of us all (Isa. 53:6).

> We may not know, we cannot tell what pains He had to
>   bear,
> But we believe it was for us He hung and suffered there.[5]
> —CECIL F. ALEXANDER (1818–1895)

Thank God for unanswered prayer. "It ain't over till it's over." God has a reason—a purpose—for all He does and all He permits. Sometimes He tells us *why* sooner than later. Sometimes we will have to wait until we get to heaven. I have no idea why God has not answered so many of my prayers. It's not over till it's over—and it will be *over* when one day God clears His name.

CHAPTER 5

ANSWERED PRAYER

*Your prayer has been heard. Your wife Elizabeth will bear
you a son... Zechariah asked the angel, "How can I be sure of
this? I am an old man and my wife is well along in years."*
—LUKE 1:13, 18

*Never give in, never give in, never, never, never—in nothing,
great or small, large or petty—never give in except to convic-
tions of honour and good sense. Never yield to force; never
yield to the apparently overwhelming might of the enemy.[1]*
—WINSTON CHURCHILL (1874–1965)

P ICTURE THIS: A young married couple named Zechariah
and his wife, Elizabeth, prayed for a child. They specifi-
cally prayed for a son. They probably did not worry too much

when that son did not come along for a while. But after two or three years perhaps they prayed with greater intensity. Then several years later—we don't know how long it was—they apparently gave up completely praying for a son. After all they were both too old, so it seemed, to be parents. They therefore assumed it was not God's will for them to have a son.

What they did not realize was that they actually prayed in the will of God the first time they asked for a son. But they apparently felt nothing. They had no idea that in heaven their prayer was heard. In any case they gave up praying. The dream was over.

Then one day Zechariah, a priest in the temple, was given a complete surprise: the angel Gabriel told him that his prayer for a son had been heard many years before. Gabriel was merely the carrier of the news. Neither Zechariah nor Elizabeth had a witness of the Holy Spirit that their prayer was heard. The first they would hear about it was when Gabriel notified them— some twenty or thirty years later!

This was not the first time Gabriel had delivered news that one's prayer had been heard without there being a previous witness of the Spirit. The prophet Daniel fasted for three weeks, not knowing whether God had taken any notice. Then after three weeks Daniel was told that God heard him the first day he started praying and fasting! "Do not be afraid, Daniel. Since the first day that you set your mind to gain understanding and to humble yourself before your God, your words were heard, and I have come in response to them" (Dan. 10:12). Note again the word heard, as we saw above, from the Hebrew *shamar*. As I said, it means God has taken our request on board and will answer it. However, He does not always give the witness of the Spirit *that* we have prayed in the will of God.

We don't usually know at first that our prayer has been *heard*. But if you do ask in God's will, He will obey your request. John does not say when God will answer you. We are only assured that *any prayer that is prayed in the will of God will be answered*. But you will ask: How do we know we have prayed in God's will? The answer is, only if the Holy Spirit witnesses this to you. That's a big *if*. This is why John adds, "And *if* we *know* that he hears us—whatever we ask—we know that we *have* what we asked of him" (1 John 5:15).

You may not have the Spirit's witness even though it was a valid request.

We are therefore dealing with two *ifs*:

1. If we pray in God's will—a very important if.

2. *If we know* that we pray in God's will.

This shows that praying in God's will and knowing you are doing this are not always the same. So John implies you can pray in God's will and not know it. Apparently Paul experienced this:

> The Spirit helps us in our weakness. We do not know what we ought to pray for, but the Spirit himself intercedes for us through wordless groans. And he who searches our hearts knows the mind of the Spirit, because the Spirit intercedes for God's people in accordance with the will of God.
> —ROMANS 8:26–27

Paul admits in these verses that he does not always know that he is consciously praying in the will of God. But when he prays in the Spirit—having no idea what he is saying—he rests on the intercession of the Spirit who certainly knows the will of God. Paul didn't know, but the Spirit knows. This also shows that the second "if" in 1 John 5:14–15 is not necessarily enjoyed by all—even the apostle Paul. I suspect therefore that knowing infallibly that you are praying in the will of God is not widely experienced.

That said, when you pray for *wisdom* you can be sure you are praying in God's will. God was pleased with King Solomon's request for wisdom when he could have asked for anything (1 Kings 3:9–10). Also James clearly told us to pray for wisdom if we lack it. So if you pray for wisdom you can be sure you are praying in God's will. And when he adds, "You must believe and not doubt" (James 1:5–6), he is essentially saying the same thing that John is saying, posing the possibility of praying with infallible assurance. Here is the thing that might be easily overlooked. James does not say that your prayer for wisdom cannot be answered; he is merely saying you don't know for sure that it will be answered.

You also know you are praying in the will of God when you pray the Lord's Prayer. For Jesus said, "This is how you should pray: 'Our Father in heaven…',", and so forth. Louise and I pray the Lord's Prayer together every day.

I suspect that most praying that has been done by the people of God was without knowing for sure that they consciously prayed in God's will. You may *think* you prayed in His will. You may *feel* you did since you know nothing that was unreasonable or unbiblical in your request. But such being the case you still don't *know* you prayed in His will.

How Do You Know God Has Heard Your Prayer?

How do you *know* you prayed in His will, that you were *heard* by the Father? The answer is: when God was pleased to give you the immediate and direct witness of the Holy Spirit that you are praying in His will; therefore it is only a matter of time that the prayer will be answered. It is a happy position to be in. I'm not sure how often it happens. My experience is that I usually feel nothing when I pray. And I normally have no idea whether my prayer is in God's will.

Here's the point: Zechariah and Elizabeth had prayed in the will of God when they asked for a son some twenty or thirty years earlier. So they were shocked when they found out their prayer had been heard. They thought it was *over* for them insofar as their heart's desire was concerned. But it wasn't over.

There is an eternal realm above—a supernatural dimension behind the scenes on earth—that is determining what goes on here below.

Have you been waiting for answered prayer? Have you given up? Could it be that in the heavenly realm, which your physical eyes cannot see, God is at work? We must fix our eyes "not on what is seen, but on what is unseen, since what is seen is temporary, but what is unseen is eternal" (2 Cor. 4:18).

It's not over till it's over. You and I are not the ones to decide when it is over. No one can decide when it's over. Circumstances don't determine when it's over. God does. He calls the shots.

Think of Things You
Used to Ask God For

Could I ask you to pause for a moment before you continue reading? Please think of things you used to ask God for. Try to come up with requests you used to share with God but gave up, assuming He would not answer your prayer—that it was *over.* May I lovingly remind you that it is not over till it's over. Until there is *no* possibility that prayer could be answered, I urge you to consider that there is still time. *It's not too late.* There was time for Zechariah and Elizabeth. Perhaps there is time for you!

I recommend that you have a prayer list—with names, conditions, or whatever is on your heart. I have used prayer lists for many years. I divide them into categories—family, friends, enemies, nations, heads of state, church leaders, persecuted Christians, health issues, unsaved friends, theological clarification regarding certain verses in the Bible, the fulfillment of certain prophecies, blessing in churches where I will be preaching, what subjects to preach on, what book to write next, and other things on my heart. I am always adding to this list, sometimes deleting items. I go through all of them daily, praying for each one at a time as though it were the first time. If you ask, How many of these are in the will of God? I have no idea. But until God indicates an undoubted, irrevocable *no*—as when a person dies or something else makes it obvious the matter is truly *over,* I keep on praying. After all, until He says *no,* the answer might be *yes.*

It ain't over till it's over.

PART II

JUMPING TO A
CONCLUSION

CHAPTER 6

THE UNSAVED

My heart's desire and prayer to God for the Israelites
is that they may be saved...Salvation has come
to the Gentiles to make Israel envious.
—ROMANS 10:1; 11:11

Each life is made up of mistakes and learning, waiting
and growing, practicing patience and being persistent.[2]
—BILLY GRAHAM

ARE YOU PRAYING for certain people to be saved? Are there those for whom you have been praying—even for a long time—but who still show no interest in coming to Jesus Christ at the moment?

Although God knows the end from the beginning, and knows

the future as perfectly as He knows the past (Isa. 46:10), should this keep us from praying for unsaved loved ones? Absolutely not. God knows what we have need of before we ask Him, but we nonetheless ask Him for what we need, for that is the way we are commanded to pray (Matt. 6:8). Likewise God knows whom He has chosen but commands us to try to save the world (Matt. 28:19). When I *witness* to people about Christ, I speak to them as if their destiny depends on them and me—knowing fully that only the Holy Spirit can convert them. I equally *pray* for those I want to become Christians as though it were up to me.

Yasser Arafat

One sunny afternoon in May 1982 Arthur Blessitt and I sat in London's Leicester Square enjoying some ice cream. Among several other things I asked Arthur to tell me about his visit with the Palestinian leader Yasser Arafat. I unexpectedly learned things about Arafat I would not have dreamed of. I can only say that I was moved to start praying for him daily—which I began doing immediately. I never thought I would meet him; I only remember feeling a burden to pray for him.

A few months after we retired from Westminster Chapel in 2002, I went to Israel to lead a tour of two hundred and fifty Brits to pray for peace. Canon Andrew White heard I was there and invited me to meet Yasser Arafat. He later said on the phone to me, "Yasser Arafat will see you in Ramallah tomorrow evening at six o'clock." I phoned Louise immediately and asked her to pray for us. Lyndon Bowring and Alan Bell had flown to Israel to spend time with me once the tour was over. I took them into Ramallah along with Andrew. It was at the time the Israelis had bulldozed Arafat's compound almost completely; no one had been allowed in—not even TV cameras. But Andrew White was the only person who had favor with both Palestinians and Israelis, and we were given permission, going through several heavily guarded checkpoints.

My first words to President Arafat were, "I'm your friend."

"You're more than a friend," he replied.

I then told him I began praying daily for him twenty years before. Tears filled his eyes. What was expected to be a fifteen-minute visit stretched to an hour and forty-five minutes. I did not go in as a politician or diplomat, but as a theologian and evangelist. Andrew said I should address him as *Rais*—the Arabic word for president.

Arafat took out his Quran and showed me that the only woman mentioned in it was the Virgin Mary. I said, "How interesting. Sounds like the Quran is indicating that Jesus is the Son of God since He had no earthly father." We spent virtually the entire time talking about Jesus Christ. Dr. Saeb Erekat, the Palestinian statesman and distinguished chief negotiator with the Israelis, sat across the table, and commented that Jesus was a prophet. I replied: "He is more than a prophet, He is the Son of God."

So Arafat quoted the Quran; I quoted the Bible. Arafat talked about Jesus ascending to heaven; I talked about Jesus dying on the cross *first*—and then ascending to heaven. Arafat talked about the plight of the Palestinians. On this I paused and sincerely commiserated with him that so many of his people had been slaughtered; I felt his pain. I added that the Israelis were spiritually blind, having generally rejected Jesus Christ as their Messiah two thousand years ago. Arafat nodded affirmatively when I said that, which I thought was interesting. But I asked him, "Where will *you* be one hundred years from now?" I added, "The most important question, Rais, is not whether you or the Israelis get Jerusalem but where will you be one hundred years from now?"

I never thought I'd meet Arafat again so I did all in my power to persuade him—then and there. I thought of what King Agrippa said to Paul, "Do you think that in such a short time you can persuade me to be a Christian?" (Acts 26:28). Paul's answer in effect was: yes! Paul tried with Agrippa; I tried with Arafat. When the visit ended, he walked outside with us. He was in no hurry for us to leave. He stayed and watched as we got into our cars. He remained there until we were out of sight, waving good-bye as the sun was setting and the Muslim call to prayer was echoing all over Ramallah. It was one of the most awesome moments of my life.

I so wanted to lead Yasser Arafat to Jesus Christ. I had good reason to believe he was more open to the gospel of Christ than most people might think. I reckoned too that if Gentiles being saved in Paul's day might provoke Israel to jealousy (Rom. 11:11), what if God would do something like this today? Call it a crazy fantasy, but what if Arafat turning to Christ led Palestinians to Jesus—and eventually Jews? I did all I could to win Arafat to Jesus.

It was not our final visit after all. I later dined with him, presented the gospel to him, took friends to Ramallah to meet him, always prayed with him—that the blood of Jesus would be sprinkled on him. Twice I anointed him with oil—making the sign of the cross on his forehead with my oily finger. I loved him, and he loved me.

Louise and I had made plans to see him in October 2004.

We were going to celebrate her sixty-fifth birthday with him in Ramallah. But he had suddenly become seriously ill. By the time we arrived in Jerusalem he was too ill to be seen. He was flown to Paris while we were in Jerusalem. On the day Arafat died a few weeks later, I wept.

I had five visits with Yasser Arafat. I had lunch with him twice. On my second visit a year later with at least a dozen members of the Palestinian Liberation Organization (PLO) present, I openly presented the gospel to him. Knowing as I did that Muslims believe Jesus never actually died on the cross—that Allah delivered Him—I urged Arafat to state publicly that Jesus Christ *died* on the cross for his sins. The translator for the members of the PLO stopped me twice, saying each time: "Stop! You are trying to convert him. You cannot do this." Both times Arafat told me to continue. Here is the gist of what I said to him:

> Rais, you are one of the most courageous men in the history of the world. But what I am asking you to do will take more courage than anything you have done—to say publicly that Jesus died on the cross for your sins. If you will do this, here is what will happen. First, you will be given a peace unlike anything you have ever experienced. Second, you will be given assurance that you will go to heaven when you die. Third, you will be given wisdom. Fourth, you will encourage Palestinian Christians, who have been so neglected. Fifth, you will send a signal to many Muslims who have had dreams about Jesus but don't know what to do with them. If you will go public that Jesus died for you, I will stand with you. I will die with you.

Andrew White wisely stepped in and changed the subject. I was afraid I had blown it, that I would never be allowed back into Ramallah. Arafat immediately assured me all is fine. Afterward Arafat's close friend and member of the PLO executive committee Dr. Emil Jarjoui came to me and said, "I have never seen our president so happy." I knew then all was indeed OK. Arafat then walked outside with Andrew and me. Arafat spoke to reporters with television cameras filming us. I phoned Louise on my cell phone and said, "Here is someone who wants to speak to you." Arafat said to Louise, "Hello, sister. We welcome your husband for peace, and hope he will come back many times."

On my third visit Alan and Lyndon went with me. Arafat provided lunch for us. Dr. Saeb Erekat joined us. Arafat would hand me food in Middle Eastern fashion. I remember him giving me a piece of broccoli. He commented that he did not eat much meat, that he was virtually a vegetarian. I said, "Rais, you don't smoke, you don't drink tea or coffee; how do you get awake?"

"Sharon!" he thundered (referring to Ariel Sharon, then the prime minister of Israel).

On my fourth visit I took Mel Gibson's film *The Passion of the Christ* into Ramallah. President Arafat and I watched the entire film together along with thirty members of the PLO, including Dr. Saeb Erekat. Arafat wept like a child throughout the film. At the point in the film when Jesus bowed His head and gave up His spirit, I whispered to Arafat: "Jesus just died." I prayed with him at the end, thanking God "for the privilege of watching the film with President Arafat." I added, "Make us thankful that Jesus Christ *died on the cross* for our sins." When I said those words Arafat squeezed my hand. I cannot be sure why he did that. To say more would be speculating.

Dr. Michael Youssef, the minister of Atlanta's Church of the Apostles, with his wife, Elizabeth, and son, Joshua, flew with me to Israel for what turned out to be my final visit with Yasser Arafat. We have most of the entire visit on film. Canon Andrew White joined us as we celebrated Arafat's seventy-fifth birthday.

I never knew for sure whether I was doing much good in those days. I had become a part of the Alexandria Peace Process, founded by Canon Andrew White and Lord Carey, recent Archbishop of Canterbury. We met a number of important people, including Shimon Peres, president of Israel. The purpose of this endeavor was to bring the religious dimension into the peace process. I reckoned then and believe now that the gospel of Jesus Christ is the only hope in the Middle East—for Jews and Palestinians. I did all I knew to do. And when Arafat died, I assumed it was *over.* I have returned to Ramallah since. Dr. Saeb Erekat kindly took me to visit Arafat's grave. I bowed my head and thanked God for the privilege I had in those days to meet President Arafat and other leading Palestinians.

I never underestimate the power of the gospel. A brief word can convert a person to Christ. So I talk to everybody for as long as I can—from heads of state to flight attendants, from Palestinians to Jews.

RABBI SIR DAVID ROSEN

A friend of mine cautioned me that if it became known that I was friendly with Yasser Arafat I would ruin my chances of reaching an Israeli. The surprising thing was that Rabbi David Rosen, a very erudite theologian and one of the most distinguished rabbis in Israel, was part of the Alexandria Peace Process. It was through this that Rabbi Rosen and I became good friends.

One morning in my quiet time while in Jerusalem, an hour before I was scheduled to have breakfast with Rabbi Rosen, an orthodox Jewish rabbi, I felt an impulse to ask him to write a book with me. I obeyed the impulse and suggested to him that I write a letter to him putting the case that Jesus is Israel's true Messiah; he could answer as he chose. We would publish our letters unedited. He agreed. Our book *The Christian and the Pharisee* (his choice for the title) was launched at Westminster Abbey in 2006.[2]

In 2005 Pope Benedict XVI awarded David Rosen with a papal knighthood; he was the first Jew ever to be given such an honor. On my website you can see a photo of David presenting Pope Benedict with a copy of our book *The Christian and the Pharisee*. In 2010 her majesty Queen Elizabeth II presented David—also an Englishman—with a knighthood, making him Rabbi Sir David Rosen.

I pray for David and Sharon Rosen every day. We stay in touch all the time. He has not been persuaded that Jesus is the eternal Son of God and Israel's promised Messiah—yet. But I shall not give up. And if I die before he embraces Jesus Christ as his Lord and Messiah, I shall pass my daily praying for him on to someone else. We are on TV together from time to time, and I say these very things to millions with him—a very gracious man—at my side. He knows I think he could be the Saul of Tarsus of the twenty-first century if he came to the Lord Jesus Christ.

It's not over until it's over.

THE PILOT LIGHTS

You may know of our Pilot Light ministry at Westminster Chapel—giving out literature about the gospel of Christ (in many languages) and talking to people about Him in the streets of Buckingham Gate and Victoria. My only regret about those twenty years of witnessing is that we did not keep detailed records of unusual conversions; they would have made such a great book and could have encouraged others to do what we did. However, although I know that what we did was a good thing to do, I never knew if we were accomplishing much. Most people refused us. I reckon that, maybe, one out of twenty accepted a tract; one out of twenty of those would listen to us present the gospel. Perhaps one out of twenty of those would pray to receive Christ. This suggests that possibly one out of sixty passers-by ended up listening to us and praying a *sinner's prayer.* Perhaps one out of twenty of them were truly saved. Who knows? But it was worth every minute.

DELAYED CONVERSIONS

A few months after we retired from the Chapel and moved to America, a letter was forwarded to me from Germany. A lady wrote to tell me that one Saturday on the steps of Westminster Chapel I gave a tract to her in the German language. She said that for years she and her family had prayed for her father to be saved. He never showed the slightest interest. But when she returned to Germany, she gave the tract to him. To her amazement he read it—and even prayed the prayer at the end of the pamphlet to receive Jesus Christ as Savior and Lord. He died the next day. It ain't over till it's over.

My wife's father did not go to church as Louise grew up. Though her mother was a devoted Christian, her dad was never interested in much that was religious. But God reached him in his old age. In the nights he could not sleep, he would turn on the television. Although he did not attend church, he *channel surfed* and watched some Christian TV programs. Once in the middle of the night he watched Jimmy Swaggart. He prayed to receive the Lord at the close of Swaggart's sermon. He died soon afterward.

A Los Angeles businessman who was Jewish attended Westminster Chapel on his way to Moscow. He was wonderfully converted. He later brought his wife, Lila, to London to meet me. I presented the gospel to her. She would not pray to receive Christ for this reason—she felt she would be agreeing that her own mother would be in hell. So she would not pray. I reasoned with her that she did not know for sure where her mother was. What if her mother picked up a Bible and read it? What if she watched a Christian program on television and invited the Lord into her heart? "What if it turns out that your mother came to the Lord before she died, and you choose to remain unsaved?" I asked. His wife sadly never came to Christ as far as I know.

But my point is this. You never know what happens to a person in their final days or hours. They could be saved at the last minute. We have a gracious God. Any word that they heard previous to their dying moment could be used by the Holy Spirit to convert them. I predict that there will be countless tens of thousands in heaven who were saved at the last minute—which no one living knew about.

Don't give up praying for the salvation of your loved ones and friends. Never, never, never, never give up!

THREE SURPRISES IN HEAVEN

Martin Luther said he expects three surprises in heaven. First, there will be those in heaven he did not expect to see there. Second, there would be those not in heaven he expected would be there. Finally, surprise of surprises, that he is there himself! Not that Luther seriously questioned whether he was saved. Dr. Martyn Lloyd-Jones always said that a Christian is a person who is surprised that they are a Christian! This is because we are all aware we don't deserve to be saved; the sheer grace of God reached us when we were unlovable and untouchable.

The truth is, whether a person was saved as a child—as I was— or converted hours before they died, as some are, such people go to heaven forever! Seventy years plus of being a Christian does not increase one's *chances*—if I may use that word; we are saved by the sheer grace of God.

One of the most disappointing eras of my life was an eighteen month period (1962–1963) when I was pastor of a small church in Carlisle, Ohio. Those were awful days. About half the church turned against me and petitioned to oust me. They only needed one more vote. But I resigned anyway and returned to Florida to sell vacuum cleaners door-to-door as I had done before. A couple who came regularly to hear me preach in Carlisle were RE (he went by his initials as I do) and Arrean. But RE was never converted. He came faithfully every Sunday to hear me. I assumed week by week that he would be the next person to be converted—if anyone was. He heard all my sermons and was always cordial, but he remained as lost as a goose! We finished our ministry there with him never being converted. We would get Christmas cards every year from them. I would write and ask if he had come to the Lord. No. I cautioned him—now in his early eighties—he surely did not have that much time. I virtually gave up on him. Lo and behold, Arrean recently wrote us that RE came to the Lord!

Deathbed Conversions

But there is more. Their son, Ron, was in his teens when we were in Carlisle. Ron came to church, but to my knowledge was never converted. A few weeks ago he found out he had a fast-growing cancer. God used this to get Ron's attention. He turned to the Lord and was saved. Just a week before I began writing this very chapter he passed away. Among his last words were: "Don't worry, Mom, we will see each other again." He was saved at last.

A greatly loved member of Westminster Chapel was a lady named Elizabeth Campbell. She and others had prayed for her husband, Sam, to be saved. But he never showed any interest in his spiritual state. He would not come to church. But he suddenly became seriously ill. One of our deacons—Benjamin Chan—visited Sam in the hospital three days before he died. Benjamin prayed with him, presented the gospel to him, and led Sam to Christ. Elizabeth was overjoyed. But weeks later she began to worry that Sam's conversion might not have been genuine; after all, he was heavily drugged when Benjamin talked with him. So she asked God to give her a sign that would give her comfort that Sam was truly saved. A children's Bible lay on the table. Elizabeth prayed and opened it. Her eyes fell on the verse that said, "The Lord revealed himself to Samuel through his word." This thrilled her to bits. But a few days after that she began to doubt it. "This was only a children's Bible, not a proper Bible," she thought to herself.

A week later we had a visiting preacher at Westminster Chapel—a man with an amazing prophetic gift. In the middle of his sermon he stopped. He looked down at Elizabeth, sitting on the fourth row. He said, "Elizabeth, you were praying in your room [he actually gave the house address and flat number]. God spoke something to you that you now fear was not really from Him. I am telling you, it *was* from Him, you can be assured of that." This prophetic man knew nothing of the previously mentioned circumstances. He only told her that what she doubted was in fact from God. Elizabeth never doubted Sam's conversion after that. It's not over until it's over.

As for deathbed conversions the thief on the cross is a biblical precedent for this. Jesus was crucified between two criminals. One of them was impudent, unkind, and insulting to Jesus. The other man, however, said to Him, "'Jesus, remember me when you come into your kingdom.' Jesus answered him, 'Truly I tell you, today you will be with me in paradise'" (Luke 23:42–43). The man was saved at the last minute. The conversion of the thief on the cross, then, is proof that a person can come to Christ on his or her deathbed. Mind you, we have only one example—that none may despair—and yet only one example—that none dare presume and take for granted they will have opportunity at the last minute.

"Now is the time of God's favor, now is the day of salvation" (2 Cor. 6:2). If the Holy Spirit is touching your heart as you read these lines, don't put it off—don't even wait until you finish this book. Stop now, bow your head and pray:

> *Lord Jesus, I need You. I want You. I know I am a sinner. I'm sorry for my sins. Wash my sins away by Your blood. I welcome Your Holy Spirit into my heart. As best as I know how, I give You my life. Amen.*

Could Yasser Arafat Have Been Saved?

The prayer just above is what I have used throughout my ministry by which many have come to the Lord. I gave this prayer to Yasser Arafat to pray before he died.

The day after Arafat died I received a phone call from Jerusalem. A lady whose name is Connie phoned to tell me that her best friend—"whom I trust totally"—had just phoned her with the following story: The previous day she had a vision around 4:00 a.m. —"Yasser Arafat is in heaven, owing to R. T. Kendall's prayers" (her words). When she turned on the television, she learned that Arafat had died in Paris at that exact time (2:00 a.m. Paris time). The same day I received another phone call from Terry Akrill, my friend from York, England. He said, "I was awakened yesterday morning at 1:00 a.m. (British time) and felt the Lord tell me to get out of bed and pray for Yasser Arafat. I had never prayed for Yasser Arafat in my life. But I did. Then the Lord seemed to say, 'You can go back to bed now.' When I turned on the television after I woke up, I learned that Yasser Arafat had died at that very moment" (1:00 a.m. in the United Kingdom, 2:00 a.m. in Paris).

I therefore have reason to believe Arafat prayed the prayer I gave him and that we will see him in heaven. Our heavenly Father is a gracious God.

It ain't over till it's over.

CHAPTER 7

HEALING

The prayer of faith will save the sick, and
the Lord will raise him up.
—JAMES 5:16, MEV

Everything is in the atonement. Jesus died for everything—the
reconciliation of all things, the resurrection of the body, the new
heavens and the new earth. The mistake some people make
is to presume a false deduction: "Therefore I can switch on
healing and claim it now." But it does not mean we can switch
on Second Coming blessings at will. Such people are over-real-
izing their eschatology and neglect the fact that we are waiting
for the physical side of salvation as in Romans 8:23. Miracles
are flashes of glory and are given in the sovereignty of God. [1]
—MICHAEL EATON

I WAS PRIVILEGED TO get to know Oral Roberts in the last years of his life. Steve Strang took me to Dr. Roberts's home in California to meet him the first time. Later I took Louise to meet him. My third visit came when I took evangelist J. John to meet him. I initially wanted to meet Oral to thank him personally for the unexpected endorsement he gave for my book *Total Forgiveness*[2] and also for writing the foreword to its sequel *How to Forgive Ourselves—Totally*.[3] He welcomed an opportunity to write the foreword for the latter book because he has had to forgive himself for certain things. In those three visits I felt I got to understand his thinking to some degree.

One of the most important things I discerned from Oral Roberts came from his telling me of an unusual experience he had a day or two before with the Holy Spirit. He said it came unexpectedly in his hallway. He took me there and showed me where it happened. He used the phrase "it was my old anointing." He said that he was shown that a very unusual move of the Holy Spirit is coming before the Second Coming and that "Israel will not miss it this time." He wept as he said this.

My point in telling the above is to note Oral's phrase "it was my old anointing." He recognized a touch of God on him in the hallway of his home that was exactly what he used to experience. He immediately recognized it. It was almost as though he had forgotten what it was like. It took him right back to the early 1950s when he saw the miraculous demonstrated time after time. There is no doubt in my mind that those miracles— people getting up out of wheelchairs, children healed, cancers healed—actually happened. Nobody made them up. This anointing, however, only lasted for a while. Then it eventually lifted—yes, from Oral Roberts. Why? You tell me. I only know that God can give or withhold mercy and if He chooses to with-hold mercy—including healing. There is nothing you and I can do to twist God's arm to make Him perform for us. We can't switch healing on at will.

I believe in divine healing. Absolutely. I believe in the mirac-ulous. I believe God can do anything. In my book *Holy Fire*[4] I sought to show that the Reformed teaching called "cessationism"—that all miracles ceased long ago—is completely false, that some good people, otherwise theologically sound, have chosen to turn a theory into a dogma. Jesus Christ is the same yesterday and today and forever (Heb. 13:8). The Holy Spirit is also the same yesterday and today and forever.

SOME PEOPLE GET HEALED, SOME DO NOT

But not all people who are prayed for get healed—even when Oral Roberts was at the height of his ministry in the early 1950s. Even in the days of the apostle Paul. Instead of praying for Timothy to be healed or telling him to believe God for his healing, Paul said to him, "Stop drinking only water, and use a little wine because of your stomach and your frequent illnesses" (1 Tim. 5:23).

And yet some people do get healed nowadays. I won't repeat the stories I related in *Holy Fire* and *The Anointing*[5]—including Louise's miraculous healing. Do read it; the accounts of healing speak for themselves.

One of the things I have learned when it comes to experi-encing any level of healing is that you should thank God for the *least* thing that happens. One problem many of us have is that we are ashamed to report a very small miracle—lest we be laughed at; we wait for the extraordinary so that the skeptics will have to believe it! But what if God gives you a small, tiny little miracle that *you* know He did but which you would prefer keep to yourself lest someone make fun of you? It is interesting to me that one of the first reported miracles of Jesus in the Gospel of Mark was a small miracle—merely of Peter's mother-in-law being healed of a "fever" (Mark 1:30–31).

Recently something happened to my right knee. I don't know what it was; I suddenly found myself limping. A year ago this happened—same right knee—and I went to my doctor. I was given an injection for pain. I had to ask for wheelchairs at airports; I preached sitting down. I had to hang on to someone when I walked. After several weeks of physiotherapy the pain subsided, and I resumed walking normally. For our six months in London Louise and I walked every day—usually for a half hour or more. Then after being back in Tennessee for two months it happened again—same knee. I have no idea what caused it. But this time it seemed worse than a year ago. By the second day I had a severe limp. It seemed far worse—and the pain was worse than the first time. I feared having to have wheelchairs again at airports and preaching sitting down. Louise asked to pray for my knee. Sure, why not? It got better in hours. Before the day was over it was good as the other knee. The pain or the limp never returned. Miracle? It was a small miracle, yes. And I am absolutely certain that God touched me.

This chapter may disappoint some readers, especially those who believe that healing is in the atonement with the same purpose and at the same level and to the same degree that salvation is in the atonement. I'm sorry, but that teaching is not true. Such a teaching is, in my opinion, misleading if not a tragic error. After I wrote the book *The Thorn in the Flesh*[6]—which was featured on the Trinity Broadcasting Network (they purchased two hundred thousand copies for pennies to give away), I received a surprising number of letters from people rebuking me for this book. Some apparently believe that everybody should be healed and believe strongly that we must uphold this point of view. One person scolded me, "Satan loves your book, man." I gather he sat under the famous prosperity teacher who said, "If the apostle Paul had my faith, he never would have had his thorn in the flesh."

It is so easy to start out with the Lord and not realize it when He chooses to go in another direction—or is for some reason pleased to withdraw His conscious presence from us. Joseph and Mary returned to their home in Galilee, thinking that Jesus was in their company. They travelled for a day without Him and then realized He was not there after all (Luke 2:43–46). Joseph and Mary did what—I fear—some of us *don't* do today. Joseph and Mary went back to Jerusalem to find Him. It took three times as long to find Jesus as it did to realize they lost Him. I wonder if high-profile people who have seen a bit of the true miraculous have the courage and integrity to admit it when the anointing *lifts*. Rather than go looking for the Lord, they keep on going, trying to convince the world they have the same anointing. Or that everyone should be healed.

The healing ministry has degenerated into a big business—a money-making enterprise in which some TV ministers exploit the financial plight of innocent people. Since I began writing this very chapter, taking a break for a cup of coffee, I turned on the television. There was a well-known person raising money to support their ministry. "This is victory over your enemy month. If you sow a seed of $229 into my ministry, you will get victory over your enemy." No mention was made of *praying* for your enemy; only victory over your enemy. I turned off the TV.

But do not despair. "It ain't over till it's over." There are several things that might follow in our day. First, God may deal with some of these people. There are many ways He could do that. Second, He may grant them repentance; they may climb down and humbly admit their folly. Third, God may resume healing people miraculously right, left, and center—any time!

In the meantime I will pray for the sick. I give appeals for healing all the time and discover, once in a while, that some people really and truly get healed. One person was healed of deafness at an Anglican church in North London—in one ear but not the other! One lady came up to me in the past year to say, "Two years ago when you were here and preached your sermon on total forgiveness, I was physically healed—right in the middle of your sermon."

I asked, "Whatever happened?"

She replied, "As you began to enumerate how we forgive and how to know we have forgiven people, I began to forgive a certain person as you spoke—and I was instantly healed." She waited two years to tell me.

God can heal anytime. He is all powerful. He is not limited by time or by our theological biases. He can use anybody—even those who are ruthless phonies. Some of them have gifts that were sovereignly bestowed on them. Such gifts are irrevocable; they come and remain without repentance, a teaching that baffles me—but I know it's true (Rom. 11:29). I don't know why Jesus chose Judas Iscariot as one of the Twelve. But He did. Apparently Judas participated in people being healed as well.

If you say these people are not worthy to have such gifts, I reply: Are *you* worthy? Who of us is?

PAUL'S THORN IN THE FLESH

We don't know what Paul's thorn in the flesh was. I have my opinion, but I don't know for sure. Whatever it was, he prayed three times for it to go away. It wouldn't leave. It was for his good. It kept him humbled. He may have wanted healing or for unscrupulous Judaizers to stop lying about him. He was only told that God's grace is sufficient for him and that he should shut up and move on. (See 2 Corinthians 12:1–9.) The truth is, we all need a thorn in the flesh—or something like that.

So do you have a thorn in the flesh? Will you always have it?

God granted me a thorn in the flesh on December 28, 1963. Few know about it. I shared it with the deacons at Westminster Chapel. I told Dr. Lloyd-Jones all about it—what it was like, when it came, and why perhaps it came. One Saturday afternoon he even laid hands on me and prayed so sweetly that it be removed. It wasn't. I still have it—after more than fifty years. Will I always have it? I hope not. But it's not over till it's over.

Do you want to be healed? Will you be healed? Don't give up. God loves to surprise. Never, never, never, never give up. Don't forget the persistent widow of Luke 18:1–8. Remember too the Greek woman who pleaded with Jesus to drive the demon out of her daughter. Strange as it may seem, Jesus was somewhat rude to her. "It is not right to take the children's bread and toss it to the dogs," He said to her. But that did not stop this lady. "Even the dogs under the table eat the children's crumbs." Then Jesus said to her, "For such a reply, you may go; the demon has left your daughter." She went home and found her child lying on the bed, and the demon gone. (See Mark 7:24–30.)

Whatever your ailment or malady, don't give up. What if

obstacles are put in your way? What if you feel that God is being unfair? Don't give up. Ask Him to heal you now.

Delayed Healing

Jennifer Rees Larcombe was paralyzed and confined to a wheelchair. She had a popular ministry all over Britain. I recall her coming to hear me preach once in Bristol. I can remember her in the front row, sitting in a wheelchair. Many people prayed for her healing. But she remained in the wheelchair and maintained her ministry. One day—out of the blue—a newly converted young lady prayed for her. After eight years of being in a wheelchair Jennifer was instantly healed! She continues her ministry everywhere—standing. Think about that. After eight years! "It ain't over till it's over."

We will all be healed after we are glorified. There will be no pain. No sadness. No disease. No thorns in the flesh. No wheelchairs.

But God can—if He wills—bring the Last Day forward, what Michael Eaton calls "flashes of glory." Are you unhappy with my expression "if He wills"? I would gently remind you that is the way the leper approached Jesus: "Lord, if you are willing, you can make me clean?" (Matt. 8:2). And that was in the day when miracles were happening under Jesus's ministry everywhere! The leper still showed respect for the sovereignty of God: "If you are willing."

If the leper could approach Jesus like that in a day when miracles were happening everywhere, how much more should you and I go to Him on bended knee and say, "Lord, if you are willing, You can heal me." All He need do is to say, "Yes, I am willing," as He did to the leper (v. 3).

I suppose I have had at least twenty people pray for my own

thorn in the flesh. Some sincere charismatics called it demon possession and supposedly cast the demon out. But whatever it is, it's still there. Will I ever be healed? I have to admit that after fifty years I have pretty much given up on this one. I assume I still need it. But I *still* hope every day that—somehow—it will go.

ONLY GOD CAN HEAL

One problem with the view that everybody should be healed because they are told healing is promised in the atonement is that when people are not healed it is supposedly owing to someone's lack of faith. The prayer of faith will save the sick. That kind of praying is when God imparts what I call *oath level faith*— when God swears on our behalf—and you *know* the person you pray for will be healed. God can give that kind of faith. But if He doesn't, we should not allow the people who are prayed for to feel guilty for their lack of faith. Or for the people who do the praying to feel guilty because people they prayed for are not healed. That to me is cruel. But the real problem with some of those who uphold the teaching that "God wants everybody to be healed" is their lack of conviction about the sovereignty of God. God said to Moses, "I will have mercy on whom I will have mercy" (Exod. 33:19; Rom. 9:15). Like it or not, He decides. Like it or not, He grants the prayer of faith to whom He will.

You cannot switch on healing at will. God does this—if He wills.

What do we do in the meantime? Ask Him. On bended knee. He may say, "I am willing." It's not over till it's over.

Finally, since Oral Roberts told me of his revelation that a major move of the Holy Spirit is coming soon that will precede the Second Coming, it is what I have been teaching for a good while. I refer to this as "Isaac" in the final chapter of my book

Holy Fire. I believe with all my heart that this mighty move of God is at hand. It will include a restoration of the gospel of Christ while also being accompanied with signs and wonders. The end will be greater than at the beginning—when the earliest church was given undoubted power.

It is truly coming. It's not over until it's over. And it is not over yet!

CHAPTER 8

THE PRODIGAL

*The father said to his servants, "Quick! Bring the best robe
and put it on him. Put a ring on his finger and sandals on
his feet. Bring the fattened calf and kill it. Let's have a feast
and celebrate. For this son of mine was dead and is alive
again; he was lost and is found." So they began to celebrate.*
—LUKE 15:22–24

*Every parent is at some time the father of the unreturned
prodigal, with nothing to do but keep his house open to hope.[1]*
—JOHN CIARDI (1916–1986)

T HE STORY OF the prodigal son is one of Jesus's best-known
and most popular parables. It is about a young man who
foolishly left home, squandered his inheritance, lived the low

life until he came to his senses and decided to return home. He feared most of all being rejected by his father, knowing as he did how he let his father down. He returned home only after hitting rock bottom. But the returning prodigal got a most spectacular, unexpected, and thrilling welcome imaginable. It is a story that speaks of God's forgiveness; a demonstration of how God accepts the greatest sinners.

It also shows how our heavenly Father welcomes the backslider home.

Are you waiting for a prodigal son or daughter to come home? Here is another relevant story that my colleague Charles Carrin shared with me:

> When I was pastor in Atlanta, I received a phone call from parents in Augusta, Georgia, whose daughter had run away from home. They had no idea where she was but knew she might have come to Atlanta. Someone had given them my name. They explained their grief and asked for help. We prayed together and after they hung up, I continued praying, asking the Lord for a "word of knowledge." Atlanta had a population of nearly two million; finding her accidentally was impossible. Almost instantly the name of a bar, which I only knew by reputation, came to my mind. Without moving from the chair, I called them and asked would they put a note on their bulletin board. It contained the girl's name and said, "You don't have to come home but please call us." The parents' names were on the bottom. That was all I did. Two weeks later a new family visited our church service. It was the parents and their daughter. They had been restored and had come to the service to share the news with me. They explained that the same day I called the bar, the girl came in and was so shocked to see the note from her parents that she

knew God was pursuing her. That fact broke through her rebellion and sent her home. Grace, as a "word of knowledge," touched her life.

Oh, the depth of the riches and wisdom and knowledge of God! How unsearchable his judgments, and his paths beyond tracing out!

—ROMANS 11:33

CHURCH LEADERS' CHILDREN

Have you ever noticed how many high-profile people in the church have experienced their children rejecting the church, family, God, and all they had been brought up to believe? Perhaps the best known is that of Franklin Graham—son of Billy—who became very rebellious, went out into the world, and turned his back on what he had been faithfully taught. But Franklin not only came back to the Lord but also has admirably succeeded his father in being an amazing preacher and has a powerful ministry that reaches around the world.

Those who have no idea what it is like to be born into the family of a preacher or church leader sometimes resent it when *children of the manse* go astray. The feeling of some is, "How could they do that? How ungrateful can people be?"

Have you any idea how hard it is for a child to grow up in the home of a pastor, vicar, or church leader? There are many reasons for this, but one of the most common is that these children are constantly being carefully observed—far more than the kids of other church members. People assume these children ought to behave better, be godlier, and should set the supreme example. Such people don't realize that being born into a godly home doesn't make you godly; being born into a manse does not necessarily give one a head start in being a Christian. First, pastors and preachers aren't perfect. Second, children being brought up in a manse, pastorium, vicarage, or parsonage are no different than anyone else. And when they make mistakes or don't perfectly epitomize Christ-centeredness, they are immediately noticed and often criticized. And those criticisms can be ruthless. The kids are sometimes crushed beyond repair.

I know. I have watched children suffer. The pain comes partly from insensitive adults and partly from their peers who are sometimes jealous. Our own children have gone through terrible times. One of them has been inflicted with a deep hurt from which they never fully recovered. It has not been easy to forgive my own enemies, but totally forgiving those who have damaged our children has been exceedingly hard indeed.

A rather funny thing took place several years ago. Dr. James Dobson, one of the most respected Christian psychologists in America, had planned to come hear me speak at Westminster Chapel. It had been arranged for Louise and me to have a meal with Jim and his wife, Shirley, afterward. I thought to myself, "Oh good. I will be able to pick Dr. Dobson's brain and get some direct help for me to know better how to handle our kids." This came when our kids were seriously struggling. The reason I call this *funny* is because I found out that the Dobsons were bringing their son to hear me, and they were counting heavily on me! They were so keen for my message to make an impact on their son! This incident made me see how all parents—no matter who they are—worries about their kids.

THE BEST OF PARENTS MAY STRUGGLE
OVER THEIR CHILDREN

I have known the best parents imaginable to have the greatest struggles and disappointments with their children and those kids have rejected their Christian heritage. I have also known parents who I thought were utterly dysfunctional, totally messed up psychologically and spiritually, but who had kids that turned out brilliantly.

My first pastor in Ashland, Kentucky, had a profound influence on me. He shaped my preaching style, motivated me to have a prayer life, and inspired me to live godly more than any other mentor since. His preaching would instill a sense of the true fear of God in the services unlike any preacher I have ever known. He himself was a great man of prayer and was the predominant influence on me to make me want to be an anointed preacher. He was a very godly man; he was my dad's hero. And yet two of his own children utterly rejected their father's church and one of them became a Mormon. This godly pastor is now in heaven. Would I be surprised if these two wayward children came back to the Lord? No, I would not. It's not over yet.

It is a common occurrence that church members unfairly have expectations of *preacher's kids* more than they do other children in a church. Those expectations put children of the manse under a lot of pressure to come up to an unrealistic standard. This is to say nothing about jealousy that some peers, for some reason, sometimes have toward preacher's children. People are people. Our children have forgiven those who may have damaged them. I dedicated my book *Total Forgiveness* to our daughter, Melissa.

We Can't Get
Past Years Back

The four of us—Louise, TR, Melissa, and I—came to live in Headington, Oxford, England, in September 1973. I will never forget the first day I went to see my supervisor, Dr. B. R. White. Among other things he said to me, "Don't forget your children. These years at Oxford will go by quickly and you won't get these years back. Don't forget your children." But I did. We had no idea of staying beyond the time it would take to finish my thesis, and I used every minute to get it written. I figured I would have time for the children when we went back to America. That was the plan. When we would say grace at the table, TR would pray, "Thank you, Lord, for the food, and help Daddy to get his DPhil so we can go back to America."

Our son TR is named for me. He is Robert Tillman II, but someone suggested we call him TR, and it stuck. He came to the Lord while he was young. I baptized him in the Kidlington Baptist Church, Oxford, when he was ten. I will never forget that occasion; it was the coldest water I was ever in—barely above freezing temperature! As a family we maintained daily devotions—reading the Bible, each of us praying daily and all of us praying the Lord's Prayer.

We moved to London in February 1977. By then TR had been put into four different schools, two of them British, two of them American (one from the US Air Force base near Oxford and one in London). TR had his difficulties. He was slightly larger than the other English boys, which did not make him popular, and they made fun of his American accent. He so looked forward to going home to America. A few days after I accepted the pastorate at Westminster Chapel, TR came to me and said, "Daddy,

you said we were going back to America, and we are still here."
I could not look at him straight in the eyes. I had no answer. I
felt horrible.

Twenty-five years later, as I relate in my book *Totally Forgiving
Ourselves*, I was asked by the Billy Graham organization to do
a video on my time in London. They asked, "Tell us about your
family and your role as a father." I replied that I would prefer
that they please talk about something else, but I said to them—
which they recorded—"On this I have been a failure. I have put
the church first, thinking I was putting God first. I put sermon
preparation first, thinking I was putting God first. I now believe
that had I put my family first I think I would have preached *just
as well*, but I can't get those years back."

When in his midtwenties TR decided to leave London and live
in America—on his own. He ended up settling in the Florida
Keys where we had spent many holidays. He seldom went to
church, and I'm afraid that God was not the center of his life.

A PROPHETIC WORD
FROM JOHN PAUL JACKSON

During this time John Paul Jackson was in London and came
into the vestry to see me. I told him about TR, wondering if
he—being well known for his prophetic gift—might have a
word concerning our son. Yes. John Paul immediately proph-
esied—although I am paraphrasing and summarizing what he
said: "TR will be the leader of the move of the Holy Spirit that
will be coming to Westminster Chapel." Really? How could
this be? TR isn't exactly living for the Lord. He isn't even living
in England! But John Paul stuck to his guns.

While TR was in Florida, Louise was touched by the ministry

of Rodney Howard-Browne. I have related her miraculous healing in other books. Rodney invited Louise to attend one of his meetings in America. It happened that he would be in Lakeland, Florida, in February 1995—a five-hour drive from where TR was now living near Key Largo. Louise asked him to fetch her while she was in Lakeland so she could spend some time with him before she came back to London. He agreed to fetch her—but only *after* Rodney's meeting was over. He adamantly refused to come to the service. But Louise begged him: "Please come for one hour and then we will go." He finally agreed. TR came to the service that began around seven o'clock. Instead of leaving after one hour, four hours later—at eleven o'clock—TR, seated up front and not wanting to leave, had totally entered right into the spirit of the entire service. He was captivated. Enthralled. They left after midnight, arriving in Key Largo at five o'clock in the morning.

But that is not all. TR inquired where Rodney would be the following week. Answer: New Orleans. TR drove to New Orleans—over eight hundred miles—the following week to hear Rodney. The day following TR's first night there, I got an e-mail from my friend Bob Ferguson who lives in New Orleans and who sat with TR at the meeting: "TR got it big time last night. He was flat out on the floor after Rodney prayed for him." TR was never to be the same again.

A few weeks after that Benjamin Chan phoned me to inquire whether TR might like to return to London. Benjamin was offering him a job working with computers. TR said yes and within a couple weeks was back at the Chapel. TR was so full of joy and excitement. He got a group of about a dozen young people together to come to our flat in Westminster to pray and worship. TR began to lead the young people on Tuesday nights at the Chapel. They began to pray for one another. On a Sunday night I invited some of the young people—mostly in their twenties—to give their testimonies at the close of the service. I then asked, "How many of you would like our young people to pray for you?" I invited all who wanted to be prayed for to make their way back to the Chapel lounge. Virtually the entire congregation came! TR led the way in praying for people, but he was helped by those same young people who had been coming to our flat each week to pray and worship. All were prayed for. A good number fell to the floor after being prayed for. What was called the *Toronto Blessing* had finally come to the Chapel. One of the group that had come to our flat to pray and worship each week was Kieran Grogan. Kieran later became our worship leader and is still the Chapel's worship leader to this day.

The following Sunday night we began praying for people after the services—along with anointing with oil for healing—in which our deacons participated. A surprising number were healed over those years after TR returned to the Chapel. John Paul had gotten it right. This pattern continued right to the close of my ministry there in February 2002.

TR and Annette married in Westminster Chapel in October 2000. Annette, who worked as an ophthalmological nurse in Moorfields Eye Hospital in London, had begun attending the Chapel a couple years before. They now have two lovely boys—Tobias Robert and Timothy Robert. They, as well as our daughter, Melissa, happily married to Rex, live near us in White House, Tennessee. I hope to one day write a book with Melissa telling her story. TR works full time with me, handling our website and books. He has traveled with me a lot—going with me all over America plus trips to South Africa,

India, Qatar, Great Britain, and China. Despite all my failures and neglect, God has restored the years which the locusts had eaten (Joel 2:25). I hope this chapter will encourage some father or mother who is waiting for your son or daughter to come home.

"It ain't over till it's over."

To God be all the praise. Another prodigal has come home.

CHAPTER 9

REVIVAL

O LORD, I have heard the report of you, and your work, O LORD, do I fear. In the midst of the years revive it; in the midst of the years make it known; in wrath remember mercy.
—HABAKKUK 3:2, ESV

There is no subject which is of greater importance to the Christian Church at the present time than that of Revival. It should be the theme of our constant meditation, preaching and prayers.[1] ... The Christian church would have been dead and finished centuries ago and many times over were it not for revivals... When the life has gone He has sent it again; when the power has vanished He sends it again. That has been the history of the Christian church from the first century until today.[2]
—D. MARTYN LLOYD-JONES (1899–1981)

SOME PEOPLE MAKE their pilgrimages to the Holy Land—to walk where Jesus walked, and I have done that many times. But I equally love to visit where the Holy Spirit has come down in historic power. Since Louise and I have retired to America, we have gone out of our way four times to a vacant lot on a corner in Enfield, Connecticut. When I go to this place in Connecticut, which is, sadly, an embarrassment to many of the people in the town, I get on my knees and pray, "Lord, do it again."

There is an engraved stone on that vacant lot that commemorates one of the most famous sermons in church history. On July 8, 1741, taking his text from Deuteronomy 32:35, "Their foot shall slide in due time (KJV), Jonathan Edwards (1703–1758) preached a sermon that lives in infamy—that is, to some. The printer named it "Sinners in the Hands of an Angry God." News of the sermon and its immediate effect went all over New England in days and all over England in weeks. It was a sermon on eternal punishment. So powerful was its affect that when he finished preaching, it was reported that people were holding on to pews in the church and tree trunks outside to keep from sliding into hell. It came at the height of America's Great Awakening.

Jonathan Edwards taught us that the task of every generation is to discover in which direction the sovereign Redeemer is moving, then move in that direction. It is a fact of church history that God does not always show up in the same way He did in a previous day. For example, what God did in the eighteenth century with George Whitefield and John Wesley in England, as well as through Jonathan Edwards in America, was unprecedented. It bore little resemblance to the way God moved, say, in the sixteenth century with people such as Martin Luther and John Calvin. But who can doubt it was the same God at work? In the sixteenth century God's move dealt mostly with doctrine—such as justification by faith alone. In the eighteenth century through Wesley and Whitefield thousands were converted in open fields—often smitten with uncontrollable manifestations.

At Westminster Chapel we prayed as a church daily for God to manifest His glory but that we all would be open to the manner in which He may choose to turn up. If we are not careful, we will put God in a straightjacket and refuse to recognize what He does unless there is a clear precedent for it—or as long as it lets us stay in our comfort zones!

WOULD YOU RECOGNIZE GOD AT WORK TODAY?

So do you believe you would recognize God at work today? Caution: God has a habit of showing up in a manner that, if we are not truly in tune with His ways, may take us by surprise—and we therefore miss Him entirely! That is what happened with the Jews in Jesus's day. Both the Pharisees and Sadducees assumed that they, if anybody, would be the first to recognize the promised Messiah. But they missed Him. Jesus wept as He looked over Jerusalem and said, "Jerusalem, Jerusalem, you who kill the prophets and stone those sent to you, how often I have longed to gather your children together" (Matt. 23:37). "If you, even you, had only known on this day what would bring you peace—but it is hidden from your eyes" (Luke 19:42).

Once when in Switzerland I visited St. Peter's Church in Geneva. I asked permission and was eventually allowed to sit in John Calvin's chair. I bowed my head and dared to ask the Lord that He might be pleased to let me be used by Him in our day as He used Calvin in his. So too when in Connecticut: I have knelt at that spot in Enfield and prayed that God would enable me to do in our day what Edwards did in his. Will those prayers be answered? Who knows? William Carey, the first modern missionary to countries outside England, used to say, "Ask great things of God; expect great things from God."[3] It's not over till it's over.

One late Sunday evening in 1956 I had a vision of great revival—revival that went right around the world. The theme of that revival was that *Jesus is coming soon,* and the surprising thing was that people everywhere believed it! They were shaken rigid. I know of no one who is shaken now and very few who believe He is coming soon. Some don't believe He is coming at all. But if that vision was truly from God, that day is coming. I believe it will be a cry that will be as real and traumatic as 9/11 and it will come in the middle of the night, metaphorically speaking, when we are in our deepest sleep—expecting nothing. I look for it daily. If I have it right, the whole church will be awakened. The true gospel will be restored. So much that has taken center stage in the church and on religious TV that is not honoring to God will be exposed and brought to nothing. Millions will be converted, including many Muslims. It will turn society upside down in a very short period of time. Finally—before the end, the blindness on Israel will be lifted and many Jews will be saved.

I thought it would have come by now. It hasn't. Yet. Perhaps it will come after I have gone to heaven. But mark it down: it's coming. The most encouraging thing I can think of at the moment is what John Wesley wrote in his journal when he saw conditions in Newcastle. He was saddened over the wickedness that prevailed in that city, adding that he had never heard such vile language in his life. He then wrote in his journal: "Ripe for revival."

MELANCHOLY CONDITIONS AT THE MOMENT

When I consider conditions at the moment on both sides of the Atlantic, I ask: Can it get any worse? Unashamed wickedness. Evil abounding. Islam growing. Innocent people being beheaded. Immorality on a widespread scale never seen in my lifetime. I think of what is available on the Internet. On television. At the cinema. The corruption in government. In politics. In business. In the banking system. In education. Marriage breakdown is on the rise more than ever. Babies are being aborted in unprecedented numbers with most people apparently feeling no conscience about it. Sexual promiscuity is out in the open more than ever—and people have become generally accepting of what goes on. Redefinition of marriage is being forced on us.

In the meantime the church is asleep. The scary thing about sleep is that you don't know you were asleep until you wake up. Also, you do things in your sleep you would not do if awake. I am sure that the church is tolerating things at the present time, whether false teachings or widespread practices, that grieve and quench the Holy Spirit. We could not bear these things if we were wide awake.

Ripe for revival? Yes. Best of all, it is surely coming. Apart from visions that other people have had—and prophecies of many people that have come from various places in the world, the Old Testament prophets have forecast that "the earth will be filled with *the knowledge of the glory of the* LORD, *as the waters cover the sea*" (Hab. 2:14, emphasis added). That day will come. The question is: Will it come before or after the Second Coming of Jesus? My view is that it will come *before*. I do not wish to enter into an eschatological discussion in this present book. I do have in mind doing that in a future book, possibly my next one, which I will call *The Midnight Cry*. I will merely state my conviction that a major move of the Holy Spirit is at hand. It will be the greatest move of the Spirit since Pentecost, eclipsing all revivals and awakenings in church history.

GOD KNOWS HOW MUCH WE CAN BEAR

But when? Soon. How long? Not long. How do I know? I don't know for sure of course. I only know what is promised in Scripture. First, that a great move of the Holy Spirit—which will go all over the world—will precede the Second Coming. I realize that the "signs of the times" (Matt. 24; Mark 13; Luke 17; 21) are put to us in a manner that could enable someone such as Jonathan Edwards to think much the same thing in his day—two and a half centuries ago. He believed that the Great Awakening in his day *was* the latter day glory of the church that some of us expect today. But, second, conditions at the present time are truly much, much worse than at any time in human history. God knows how much we can bear. There is an aspect of God's ways that is relevant here. He will not allow horrible and painful things to go on and on indefinitely or let His people suffer on and on without a letup, "for then the spirit [of man] would grow faint before me" (Isa. 57:16, ESV). Furthermore, things will be so awful, said Jesus, that the days will be "cut short." "If those days had not been cut short, no one would survive, but for the sake of the elect those days will be shortened" (Matt. 24:22). We are surely right on the brink of this. I can only trust that God will step in soon. Third, some of my own unfulfilled visions encourage me to believe that the next great move of God is at hand. But I have to add: it will be accompanied with great suffering. There will be great power, yes. It will be the greatest outpouring of the Spirit since Pentecost. It will include many healings and miracles. But the kind of persecution that most of us have only read about—as in Egypt, Syria, and Iraq—will come to the West. Are we ready for this?

Perhaps I will be forgiven for having hoped that this revival I am still expecting would have—in some measure—come to Westminster Chapel while I was there. I thought I would surely see the beginnings of this great revival. It was a hard decision to announce our retirement, but I reasoned that twenty-five years was long enough. Even after I gave them a thirteen-month notice I hoped it might still come—right up to my last Sunday—and keep me there a while!

But I came to terms that it was *over*—at least revival coming while I was at the Chapel. At the close of our final Sunday morning sermon we sang Graham Kendrick's hymn, "For This I Have Jesus." The future was so uncertain. I was unknown in America. I would leave London, accepting the disappointment that revival had not come. But for this I have Jesus. I was not prepared for its effect on me. I sat down and wept while Robert Amess, who joined me in the pulpit for that final Sunday, closed the service.

It's hard to come to terms with the realization that something you so earnestly hoped for is truly *over* when you were anticipating a different outcome.

However, I haven't given up on seeing the beginnings of this coming move of the Holy Spirit somewhere in the world. I don't know for sure where it will first break out. What I envisage is not just *another revival* but *the* awakening of awakenings—forecast in Matthew 25:6—when the wise and foolish virgins were awakened. It is my view that this awakening will precipitate this great revival.

IMAGINED VISIONS

One of the things one often faces when it comes to future out-pourings of the Spirit is that so many of them are thought to come to one's own area. Some Americans believe the next great move of the Spirit will come to America; some Brits believe it will come to the United Kingdom. So too with other places in the world; all those who have been seeking the Lord believe the Lord has shown them that God will come to their own land. I have an e-mail from one person who had a vision that *proves* that the next great move of God will come to the little village of Rush, Kentucky. I heard a lady prophesy in 1956 that the greatest revival in church history would come to a certain tabernacle in Ashland, Kentucky. I googled this little church and discovered it still exists. So maybe it will still come there?

The world of visions, revelations, and prophetic words is filled with many bizarre notions, strange ideas, and personal hopes—so often based upon what one so wishes for. It would be easy to become cynical and adopt a cessationist point of view so that in one stroke you could dismiss the entire lot as totally false. That would be the easy way out. I have enough information regarding the counterfeit that could possibly vindicate many a cessationist! In a former church I was in, there was a sincere lady whose baby was born with a cleft palate. But she had a vision that her child would be healed. Consequently she refused to submit to surgery that would have taken care of the problem. The healing never came. The poor child grew up with the uncomfortable malady for the rest of his life.

Good, sincere, God-fearing, and Bible-loving people have imagined visions, revelations, and prophetic words that were obviously not from God. But some strange manifestations have occurred in church history, believe it or not, that have been from God! When George Whitefield preached in the fields in England—going against all tradition, there were extraordinary outpourings of the Holy Spirit. Hundreds and hundreds were converted. England was all the better for it, as even secular historians have shown. But in this same move of the Holy Spirit there were also all sorts of peculiar manifestations—people shrieking, falling, barking like dogs, weeping, and laughing. John Wesley rebuked Whitefield and told him to stamp out the false manifestations. Whitefield agreed with Wesley that much indeed was of the flesh, but he also believed that if one tries to stamp out what is false you will destroy what is real with it. Therefore one must leave things. Wesley himself ended up preaching in the fields and saw the same unusual manifestations.

When I recognize the possibility of sincere people having visions that are not from God, who is to say that any of us is exempt from having the same? So who am I to claim that my own vision of worldwide revival was of *God*? Am I capable of having a vision or prophecy that is based upon personal aspiration? I certainly am.

Then why should I even talk about it? I reply: I am willing to pass on what I saw and then to wait and see. As Paul said, "Judge nothing before the appointed time; wait until the Lord comes. He will bring to light what is hidden in darkness and will expose the motives of the heart. At that time each will receive their praise from God" (1 Cor. 4:5). The words "wait until the

Lord comes" no doubt refer to the Second Coming. But I don't hesitate to apply it to *any* manner in which the Lord can show up and at any time when He may choose to step in and make things clear.

What hope then have I that my vision of revival that swept around the world was from the Holy Spirit and not my own wish? I would hang on to two things:

1. The Old Testament prophecies that refer to the glory of the Lord covering the earth as the waters cover the sea

2. My exegesis of the Parable of the Ten Virgins

But even if I am correct in the way I apply *both* of these two categories, such a revival could still come after I die. It is possible that God truly showed me things that are coming, but this could still be a phenomenon in which I have no part at all.

I can live with that. I gave up hope that revival would come to Westminster Chapel while I was there, and I am prepared to take the same stance regarding the latter day glory of the church generally.

We cannot claim to be devoted to the glory of God if we are not equally willing *not to be a part* of what we hoped we would be a part of. It is His glory we must pursue. One of my earlier mentors Dr. N. B. Magruder—who preached my ordination sermon in November 1964—wrote a note to me that shook me to my fingertips: "My willingness to forsake any claim upon God is the only evidence I have seen the Divine glory." A profound, soul-searching, and God-honoring statement.

We must remember that it is not always about us.

CHAPTER 10

TEN SECONDS
BEFORE MIDNIGHT

It is my son's robe! Some ferocious animal has devoured
him. Joseph has surely been torn to pieces...I will con-
tinue to mourn until I join my son in the grave.
—GENESIS 37:33, 35

It was the best of times, it was the worst of times.[1]
—CHARLES DICKENS

I WILL NEVER FORGET it as long as I live. It was one of the
most harrowing moments of my life. I was driving on
the only road that leads from the mainland of Florida into
the Florida Keys, Route US 1—a straight eighteen-mile, two-
lane highway, famous for being one of the most dangerous

highways in America.[2] TR had gone ahead of me in his small two-door silver hatchback Honda. Suddenly the traffic came to a complete halt. Fifteen minutes later I heard the siren of an ambulance. It passed me, going in the direction of Key Largo. I immediately feared the worst—that TR had been in an accident. No information came for what seemed like an eternity. Then someone who had a cell phone said that a young person a couple miles up the road was dead. I was now in an acute state of anxiety. Another report came that it was a young man driving a small two-door hatchback silver Honda. It had to be TR. How many young men would be driving a small two-door silver Honda in that eighteen-mile stretch? As soon as I could, I stopped a policeman and asked if he had any information. He only knew that a young man driving a silver two-door hatchback Honda was just killed in an accident. I thought I would die on the spot. My heart began beating as if it would come out of my chest. I said to the policeman that I am pretty sure that it is my own son who is dead. He asked me my son's name. He called ahead. The man who was dead was not my son.

I was suddenly the most relieved and thankful man on the planet. Never was I so sure of anything—that my son had been taken out of this world. I was wrong. I had jumped to a conclusion based upon most convincing evidence. But I was completely wrong.

Jumping to a false conclusion is an easy thing to do. High-powered lawyers convince juries too often with what at first seems to be irrefutable evidence, but sometimes it eventually turns out that justice was not done after all. Doctors make faulty diagnoses based upon insufficient medical evidence. More than twenty years ago Louise was scheduled to have a major operation in London's Westminster Hospital, but another doctor, a close friend, convinced her in the nick of time to get a second opinion. It turned out that there was nothing wrong with Louise at all!

Bankers misjudge customers and the value of assets and make bad loans. Publishers have been known to turn down a book that they thought would be a financial disaster, only to have a different publisher to turn the same book into a best seller.

When you have been falsely accused, and everyone believes the lie, you might feel there is nothing to live for. When you are told you have a short time to live, based upon certain evidence, you might feel there is nothing to live for. When you have lost your job, home, filed for bankruptcy, and have no one to turn to you may feel there is nothing to live for.

WE ALL NEED SOMETHING TO LIVE FOR

We all need to have something to live for, something to look forward to, having friends that know all about us and still love us. Yes, a good relationship with God may well compensate for the bleakest kind of outlook, but most of us need more than a close walk with God in order to be reasonably happy. I will quote it again: "[God] knows how we are formed; He remembers that we are dust (Ps. 103:14, MEV).

Take loneliness. Even *before* the Fall of Adam and Eve God had said it is not good for man to live alone (Gen. 2:18). So how much more painful is it when we have a sinful nature to contend with? I remember hearing a song titled "How Can I Be Lonely," which suggests that I can't be lonely since I have Jesus, surely an unrealistic expectation. For the answer is: you certainly *can* be lonely—even when you have Jesus only.

There was a very nice American lady who came to Westminster Chapel for several years. A lady in her late forties she was faithful in supporting the Chapel and was a tremendous blessing to everyone. But one day she decided her time in London was up. Louise and I were invited to her flat for a meal on the night before she was to return to Arkansas. Just before we left, I was asked to pray. A second before I began to pray I asked her as sensitively and gently as I knew how, "Mary, would you like to be married?" Although she had completely given up on the idea, she replied, "Yes I certainly would." I then prayed that God would lead her to a man who wants her as much as she wants him. The next day she was met at the plane in Little Rock by a man who was asked at the last minute, almost accidently, to pick up someone at the airport. He did. It was love at first sight for both of them. They married six months later!

GOD WANTS YOU TO HAVE SOMETHING TO LIVE FOR

God wants you to have something to live for. If you are single, who am I to say to you that you have Jesus and He is enough? For some, yes. For others, you want to be married. It is easy for me to say—not having to experience singleness for a long time—but I will nonetheless suggest as caringly and lovingly as I can that it is still true: no good thing will God withhold from them who desire to please God (Ps. 84:11). God *will* compensate somehow. He knows how much we can bear (1 Cor. 10:13). It's not over till it's over. Who knows what God might have in mind for you?

The Bible contains stories of people who prematurely jumped to a wrong conclusion, but which was based upon *irrefutable* evidence.

For some twenty years David spent his time doing nothing but running from King Saul. He lived this way day after day for all those years—just to stay alive. But he eventually came to the end of his tether. He became so discouraged that he concluded—despite having been anointed by Samuel—that he would not survive. "One of these days I will be destroyed by the hand of Saul" (1 Sam. 27:1). Sometime after that, still on the run from Saul, even David's closest supporters turned against him. David hit rock bottom. Some of his men were talking of stoning him. David—alone—"strengthened himself in the LORD his God" (1 Sam. 30:6, ESV). It wasn't over for him. By appealing to what he knew about God and His faithfulness, David was able—by God's help—to pull himself together in the darkest hour of his life. He knew again he had something to live for.

Then there was Elijah. Despite his major triumph over the prophets of Baal on Mount Carmel, Elijah ran out of steam. He let Queen Jezebel intimidate him. He ran for his life. Elijah too hit rock bottom. He felt he had nothing to live for. "I have had enough, LORD...take my life" (1 Kings 19:4). But God stepped in. God wasn't finished with him yet. There was still more work for Elijah to do.

The prophet Jeremiah became so discouraged that he cursed the day he was born (Jer. 20:14). He said to God, "You deceived me, LORD, and I was deceived" (v. 7). But God came to Jeremiah's rescue, vindicating his prophecies in the end after all Israel had accused him of treason.

So if David, the only man in the Bible called a man after God's own heart (Acts 13:22), could sink so low emotionally, if Elijah, one of the greatest prophets of the Old Testament, could ask God to take his life, and if Jeremiah, a prophet who had been called from his mother's womb (Jer. 1:5), could become so discouraged that he would curse the day he was born, should you and I be surprised if we too are tested to the hilt?

The Best of God's People Get Discouraged

The truth is, the best of God's people get very, very discouraged. Charles Spurgeon frequently suffered from depression. He was the greatest preacher of the nineteenth century. William Cowper suffered from what is now called *bipolar disorder*. And yet in deep distraught Cowper wrote such hymns as "God Moves in a Mysterious Way" and "There Is a Fountain."

Our twenty-five years at Westminster Chapel were filled with agony and ecstasy, anxiety and joy, expectation and bleakness. "It was the best of times, it was the worst of times," to quote Charles Dickens. There was a moment in which I alerted one of our deacons that I might have to announce our resignation and return to America—things were so bad. I will never be able to write more than what I relate below; the matter is still too sensitive. I can only report that God was with us "through it all"—to quote the title of one of Andre Crouch's lovely hymns. The well-known bass singer Frank Boggs showed up one evening at the Chapel. I invited him to sing. He kindly obliged, not knowing how much Louise and I needed to hear the words of that song at that very moment.

Yes, there were times Louise and I felt we had nothing to live for. It was that bad.

There were actually several moments I thought "it's over." But I will share this one. The night of January 16, 1986 was the *night of nights*—a church meeting at Westminster Chapel. Without doubt it was the most memorable in its history. Things came to a head after nearly four years of turmoil—all owing to my inviting Arthur Blessitt to speak for us for six weeks during April and May 1982. It was the best decision I made in twenty-five years, but it led to one of the greatest trials of our lives. Arthur ruffled the feathers of some of our deacons. At first it was only one deacon; three years later it was six. I would have been forgiven for having Arthur had I gone back to *business as usual* when he moved on. But my *crime* was that I kept up most of the things Arthur started. I continued giving a public appeal for people to receive Christ. We began singing choruses as well as the old hymns. We began our Pilot Light ministry—giving out tracts and witnessing in the streets of Westminster between Buckingham Palace and Victoria Station.

Had I never invited Arthur Blessitt to preach for me, no deacon or member of the Chapel would have taken notice of a particular review of my book *Once Saved, Always Saved*.[3] But the six deacons who opposed my ministry felt it was time for me to move on. But how to achieve this? They decided to accuse me of heresy—antinomianism, as charged by a Reformed magazine. Antinomianism (lawlessness) is popularly conceived to mean that since you are saved you don't have to keep the works of the Law.

The Sunday before Christmas 1984 I was presented with a letter that would be sent immediately to all members of the Chapel. The six deacons had signed a letter in anticipation of the January church meeting. They attached a copy of the *Banner of Truth* review of *Once Saved, Always Saved*.

I Thought My Ministry Was Over

I will never forget that Christmas. It was difficult to enjoy watching our children opening their presents. Louise had prepared her usual turkey dinner, but we had little appetite. I went to bed nightly with the realization that if those six deacons got their way, I would not only have to resign as minister of Westminster Chapel but also possibly be out of the ministry entirely. We would have to return to America in disgrace—with no future in the ministry.

Indeed, unless God intervened, it was *over* for us at the Chapel. For when a church like Westminster Chapel—known everywhere for its evangelical orthodoxy—accuses one of heresy, it is a very serious charge indeed. So how can that ministry survive? Who would trust us? Who would believe us? I dreamed almost every night of selling vacuum cleaners door to door—something, you may recall, I had done years before. I would have dreams of going back to the Miami store, packing vacuum cleaners into my car to sell. I would dream of knocking on doors in Miami Beach, Coral Gables, Pompano Beach, and Fort Lauderdale. My career as a respected minister would be *over—kaputt—*if these six deacons persuaded 51 percent of the members that I was a heretic. My reasoning and fears may have been exaggerated; perhaps there would have been a church in America who would have me. But there is no doubt that the stigma on me would never be erased, whether in America or Britain.

At the church meeting on January 16, 1985, I asked my assistant, Jon Bush, to preside. Lloyd-Jones Hall was packed. People showed up who were on the membership roll but who never heard me preach. Mr. Ernest Paddon, a deacon and loyal supporter, made a motion that the six opposing deacons withdraw their accusation or resign. The motion was seconded. The debate began. Mr. M. J. Micklewright, known as the Chapel patriarch, stood up on behalf of my ministry and quoted Dr.

Martyn Lloyd-Jones: "If our preaching is not accused of being antinomian it is probably because we haven't really preached the gospel."

But after Mr. Micklewright sat down, our supporters largely went quiet. Those who opposed me—one after another— spoke, supporting the six deacons. Virtually no one who supported my ministry stood to speak. One lady began praying the Lord's Prayer aloud. It helped ease the tension. Others joined her. Someone suggested that there be a recess. Perhaps the six opposing deacons would change their minds? The meeting stopped for a twenty-minute recess.

It seemed *over*. There was little doubt about it. Those members who stood up and spoke against us had, I assumed, persuaded every member present to support the opposing six deacons. I imagined the four of us getting on a plane the next day—heading back to America. In much the same way as believing that the man in the two-door silver hatchback Honda was our son, I jumped to a conclusion. I looked back at Louise, sitting right behind me. TR was at her side. I was hoping to get assurance from her. She was looking for assurance from me. She shrugged her shoulders as if to say, "It's all over." I knew it was over. My ministry at the Chapel was over. I just stared at the floor. All of a sudden—out of the blue—I had a vision: at my right hand, it seemed like inches away, was a pillar of fire. I heard a voice clearly: "Do not lean on your own understanding but trust in the Lord with all your heart." That gave me hope in that heavy moment. I have wondered why God did that—He knew what the turnout would be a few minutes later. Amazing.

The six opposing deacons returned to Lloyd-Jones Hall. Jon Bush asked them if they had changed their opinion. No.

A member stood up and said: "I move that we vote" (that is, vote on the motion that the six deacons withdraw their charges against me or resign). The motion was seconded. Secret ballots were passed out. Four people—called *scrutineers*—had been asked to count the ballots. About thirty minutes later they returned with the vote count: the overwhelming majority (2–1) voted that the opposing six deacons should resign.

We survived. The long nightmare was over. We still had a future at the Chapel.

Terry Akrill, now in heaven, was a very humble lay member of St. Michael le Belfrey of York, England. I have written about him in two of my books, calling him the most supernatural person I have ever met. For some reason Terry was gripped by the idea of *time.* "Time is God's domain," he would say to me. This means God gives all of us enough time to do what we need to do. This also means that God can show up anytime He pleases. It is therefore God's prerogative to step in at the very last minute. "Sometimes God likes to do things ten seconds before midnight," he once said to me.

As far as I was concerned, God showed up ten seconds before midnight at that historic church meeting at Westminster Chapel.

Therefore until it is truly midnight, we should not give up. After all, it ain't over till it's over.

JACOB THOUGHT IT WAS OVER FOR HIS SON JOSEPH

When Jacob saw Joseph's coat that had been soaked in blood, he jumped to a conclusion: "Joseph has surely been torn to pieces" (Gen. 37:33). Jacob tore his clothes, put on sackcloth, and mourned for his son. "All his sons and daughters came to comfort him, but he refused to be comforted... 'I will continue to mourn until I join my son in the grave'" (vv. 34–35). The truth is that the other sons of Jacob had sold Joseph to the Ishmaelites, never expecting to see him again. God, however, was with Joseph. Joseph survived false accusations and eventually became the prime minister of Egypt. He sent for Jacob and all the family to come and live in Egypt.

Hebrews 11 is the well-known *faith* chapter of the Bible; many of the Old Testament stalwarts are acknowledged for their faith. But Jacob, whose name appears in the Old Testament more than all the others, only gets one mention: "By faith Jacob, when he was dying, blessed each of Joseph's sons, and worshiped as he leaned on the top of his staff" (v. 21). Jacob was a very, very grateful man. He had given up hope of ever seeing his son Joseph again. He was gloriously wrong.

But is there hope for those who have messed up—seriously messed up? Do you fear you are *yesterday's man* or *woman*?

DO YOU FEAR YOU HAVE NOTHING TO LIVE FOR?

There are two kinds of *yesterday's* men or women:

1. When you are finished in the sight of God

2. When you are finished in the eyes of people

If you are finished in God's eyes, I'm sorry, but it is *over.* Even if the people think you are wonderful. That is the way it was with King Saul. He had been rejected by God, but only Samuel knew it (1 Sam. 16:1). You may read my book *The Anointing* for the details. Saul had put himself above Holy Scripture. He refused to listen to Samuel or be accountable. He never truly repented. He lost all integrity. And yet in the eyes of the people he remained king for another twenty years. I truly fear there are people like that in the ministry today.

And yet there are those who are rejected by the people who may not be rejected by God. The people see them as *yesterday's* men or women. But not God. What He thinks is all that matters.

Here's my take on whether a person who has seriously messed up still has a future: Will he or she get right with God if they *still* don't get their old position back? If your repentance is carried out *only* on the condition that you get your previous position or ministry back, I'm afraid I would have to call it a spurious repentance. But if you are prepared to live sexually pure, be squeaky clean when it comes to money matters, and dedicate your heart and soul to the honor and glory of God *without* getting your job or ministry back, there is hope for you. God wants you to have something to live for.

I cannot imagine anybody messing up more than Samson. He showed no will power, no discipline; he was easy prey for the opposite sex. He fell. It was terrible. The anointing was lifted from him right after he foolishly revealed the secret of his strength to beautiful Delilah. His enemies gouged his eyes out. If ever there was one who appeared to be yesterday's man, it was Samson. Little doubt about that.

But his hair began to grow. Though blind and despised, he came back—strong enough to accomplish more at the end of his life than in all the rest of his life (Judges 16:30). Samson was yesterday's man in the eyes of people, but not in the eyes of God. Think about it—he is even mentioned in Hebrews 11:32! Would *you* have listed Samson as a man of faith? I doubt I would have.

But God had not completely left Samson. His work was not finished after all.

It's not over until it's over.

Most of us would have jumped to the conclusion that Samson had no future, just as Jacob wrongly assumed he had nothing to live for.

David hastily concluded that he had no future. But he "encouraged himself" in the Lord his God. There is a happy future for a person like that.

PART III

THE FAITHFULNESS OF GOD

CHAPTER 11

THE GOSPEL

*For I am not ashamed of the gospel, because it is the power
of God that brings salvation to everyone who believes: first
to the Jew, then to the Gentile. For in the gospel the righteousness of God is revealed—a righteousness that is by
faith from first to last, just as it is written: "The righteous will live by faith." The wrath of God is being revealed
from heaven against all godlessness and wickedness of
people, who suppress the truth by their wickedness.*
—ROMANS 1:16–18

*If your preaching of the gospel of God's free grace in Jesus Christ
does not provoke the charge from some of antinomianism, you're
not preaching the gospel of the free grace of God in Jesus Christ.*[1]
—D. MARTYN LLOYD-JONES (1899–1981)

I N A MIDWEEK service at Calvary Church of the Nazarene in Nashville, Tennessee, on December 2, 1954, I preached my first sermon. My text was from Lamentations 3:23: "Great is thy faithfulness" (KJV). I preached all I could think of on that subject. My sermon lasted eighteen minutes.

If you were to ask me what is the most wonderful thing I know about God, it is this: He is faithful. As Paul said, "God is faithful, who has called you into fellowship with his Son, Jesus Christ our Lord" (1 Cor. 1:9). Faithfulness means keeping your word. God keeps His word. He is faithful in all He has promised. The Bible is God's integrity put on the line. It is impossible for Him to lie. Truth is what He is.

I am amazed that we have a God like this. When I ponder this it sometimes takes my breath away. He is perfect in every way. He is unimprovable. If I were given the option of changing God—or changing what I don't like about Him—I can tell you that there is nothing I would add or take away from the way He is. Here's the thing. He did not make Himself that way. That is the way He *is*. This is what I find so amazing. What if you and I were left with a God we don't like—and there was nothing we could do about it? If we were invited to *create* what we believe would be the perfect God—the best, the most wonderful and glorious God imaginable, what kind of God would you come up with? Would He be different than the God of the Bible?

As we come toward the end of this book, I am saying—after seventy-four years of being a Christian, sixty years as a minister of the gospel, and more than fifty-seven years of marriage—that the God of the Bible is a greater God than I could have imagined. I have no complaints to make with Him. None.

Does this mean I understand all His ways? No. Does this mean I like everything He permits? No. Does this mean I am thrilled with everything His word teaches? No.

Here is my reasoning: what I know about God is so wonderful that I can only conclude that what I don't know is equally good. If you ask, "What is it that you don't understand about God?" I answer: I don't know fully why He allows evil. I don't understand the teaching of eternal punishment. I don't know why He took my mother to heaven when she was only forty-three and I was seventeen and my little sister was only two. I don't know why He has let some of the people I admired the most let me down.

If you ask me whether I expect to understand the reasons for these things one day, I answer *yes*. I don't expect to learn *all* there is about God—ever. He is infinite. We will be learning more and more and more about Him throughout eternity. But I am convinced I will be satisfied with what I learn.

After Dr. Martyn Lloyd-Jones went to heaven in 1981, I continued to be Mrs. Lloyd-Jones's pastor until she died ten years later. We spent many hours together. When discussing the issue of eternal punishment one day, she said to me, "I always lean on Genesis 18:25 for things about God I don't understand— Will not the Judge of all the earth do right?'"

WHATEVER HAPPENED TO THE GOSPEL?

At my farewell service at Westminster Chapel in 2002 I made this comment: "Whatever happened to the gospel?" I asked this because I have been very worried how the gospel seems to have passed behind a cloud—both in Britain and in America. I am troubled that some people in the church seem to be interested in nearly everything else but the gospel. But equally alarming is what I perceive as a very subtle departure from the gospel by some high-profile people.

Let us suppose that a jet takes off from New York's JFK airport and a couple minutes later the pilot notices that the plane is off course by a very small degree. What if the pilot says to himself, "This is a very small degree off course; I will sort it out later." But if it is not sorted out immediately, seven hours later the same plane will be circling over Spain rather than London's Heathrow airport.

That, in my opinion, is what has happened on a large scale when it comes to understanding the gospel of Jesus Christ at the present time. The slightest deviation from the gospel as Paul articulated it seems innocent to many. But down the road there is a price to pay—a supreme price, namely, that the gospel is almost unrecognizable in some places.

I write this chapter partly out of my concern for the church of tomorrow. If I could choose my legacy it would be that I helped to stop a trend that was moving away from the gospel of the New Testament.

When I ponder the faithfulness of God in my life, one of the things for which I am *most* thankful is that the gospel of Jesus Christ was indelibly imprinted on my mind many years ago—but not from my old denomination. And yet Dr. Martyn Lloyd-Jones used to say that my Nazarene background is what saved me from being "perfectly orthodox, perfectly useless." True. But he would never have put me in Westminster Chapel had I not been *perfectly orthodox*, I can safely tell you. Before I met Dr. Lloyd-Jones—but subsequent to my Trevecca days—I was given grace to understand the gospel as taught by the apostle Paul. This actually came by direct revelation of the Holy Spirit and reading the Bible. But it was confirmed by faithful teaching of certain mentors such as Henry Mahan, N. Burnett Magruder, and Rolfe Barnard. I was taught the gospel so well in the years 1956–1957 that I became able to detect the slightest deviation from it. Sometimes I think I can smell heresy coming a mile away.

I was brought up in a denomination that stressed godliness more than God and holiness more than the gospel. The consequence of this was that I grew up believing I would go to heaven as long as I was walking in sanctification. This is no doubt why I am overly sensitive regarding any teaching that attaches the necessity of good works as a condition of salvation. But when I went to Southern Baptist Theological Seminary in 1971, I was confronted with a different set of challenges—ranging from universalism to existentialism, from Barthianism to open theism. God was exceedingly gracious to me—preserving me from theological pitfalls that would have wrecked my ministry.

WHAT IS THE GOSPEL?

So let me explain what I mean by the *gospel*. It is the good news that *faith alone in Christ alone* guarantees that you will go to heaven when you die. *Faith in Christ plus nothing saves you.* The righteousness of God is put to your credit when you rely only on the blood of Christ.

When Paul says that in the gospel there is a righteousness revealed "from faith to faith" (Rom. 1:17, MEV), he means that the faith *of* Jesus Christ must be ratified—put into effect—by *our* faith. In other words, God's righteousness is revealed from *Christ's faith to our faith.* The two together save us. Had Paul merely said that the righteousness of God is revealed by *the* faith of Jesus Christ—full stop, it would have meant that we do not need to believe; it would mean that Jesus believed for us.

And yet Jesus *did* believe for us. But that is not enough. We too must believe or all He did for us is of no value. Therefore, the reason Paul says "faith to faith" is because it was not enough for Christ to believe for us; we too must believe.

A major learning experience came to me during my Oxford *viva voce*—oral exam. DR. T. H. L. Parker, probably the best-known Anglican Barthian and a translator of Calvin's commentaries, was one of my examiners at my *viva*. He commented to me during my *viva* that my thesis—published later as *Calvin and English Calvinism to 1648*—showed him the difference between Karl Barth and John Calvin. Although this was not something I had set out to prove, for Dr. Parker this was important. Barth was a universalist but always claimed to be following Calvin. But Calvin was no universalist. Calvin taught that all that Christ did in dying for the salvation of the human race was of "no value" until *we* believe.

Salvation comes "through *faith* in his blood" (Rom. 3:25, KJV, emphasis added). Faith is resting your case solely upon the work of Jesus Christ—His sinless life and sacrificial death. The moment you transfer your hope in what you do for God to what He has done for you, the righteousness of God is put to your credit. This imputed righteousness cannot be forfeited. Once justified, always justified; once saved, always saved. This is what set me on fire! When I saw this, I never looked back; I have never gotten over it. It not only gave me an assurance of my eternal salvation, which has never wavered, but it also provided a theological foundation that has enabled me to weather many an intellectual storm. Intellectual temptation is like sexual temptation; you never know how strong you will be. What has saved me is seeing what Jesus Christ did. Once that is grasped, we are less likely to fall for any alteration of Paul's gospel.

Paul quotes Habakkuk 2:4: "The just shall live by faith," in Romans 1:17 (KJV). The reason Paul uses the phrase "faith to faith" in Romans 1:17 is because the Hebrew in Habakkuk 2:4 refers to the faithfulness of God. Habakkuk 2:4 is probably best translated, "The just shall live by His faithfulness"; we live by *God's* faithfulness. Therefore living by His faithfulness in Habakkuk's day becomes living by "*the faith* of the Son of God" (Gal. 2:20, KJV). Indeed, Paul says that we believe "in" Jesus Christ in order that we might be justified "by the faith *of* Christ" (v. 16, KJV). Paul quotes Habakkuk 2:4 in order that we might know the background for his phrase "faith to faith." Therefore in the same way that the faithfulness of God must be matched by our faith, so too the faith, or faithfulness, of Christ must be ratified by our faith—or His atonement is of no value. This is precisely what exposes the Barthian error.

When I preached my first sermon on the faithfulness of God in 1954 I could not have known how essential the faithfulness of God is to Christ's atonement. When I first started preaching, I accepted Arminian-Wesleyan teaching uncritically, having no thought of getting out of that theological box. Later on I came to see that the faithfulness of God—that is, the faithfulness or faith of His Son Jesus Christ—is what saves us. And yet it is of no value unless we rely on His faith.

WHY SHOULD A PERSON BE A CHRISTIAN?

But there is one more thing that is crucial. Paul hastens to give the reason for the urgency of this gospel: "for" (Greek *gar*). Why must we believe? Why be a Christian? The answer is: "*For* [because] the wrath of God is revealed" (Rom. 1:18, KJV).

Does this surprise you?

Paul gives his reason why a person should be a Christian. Do you think that Paul would not agree with the view, "If there were no heaven or no hell I would still be a Christian"? No, says Paul. On the contrary, he says that if in this life only we have hope in Christ we are to be pitied (1 Cor. 15:19)!

Why should a person be saved? What would you say is the reason a person ought to be a Christian? Is it because it will help their marriage? Is it because they will be happier in life? Is it because God will consequently come to their aid in finances?

Paul gives the reason right at the beginning of Romans, his longest letter and the one in which he gives the most detailed description of the gospel. It is *because of God's wrath—His anger with sin.* God sent His Son into the world because of the sin of all humankind. So those who believe in Jesus Christ will "not perish"—a reference to eternal punishment—but have eternal life (John 3:16). We are justified by Christ's blood in order to be "saved from God's wrath" (Rom. 5:9). It is Christ who "rescues us from the *coming wrath*" (1 Thess. 1:10).

How God Ultimately Punishes Sin

There are essentially two ways by which God ultimately punishes sin:

1. By the blood of Jesus

2. By everlasting punishment in hell

One of my old mentors Rolfe Barnard used to say, "The fires of hell and the blood of Jesus go together." The justice of God is satisfied completely by the blood of Jesus. Hell does not truly satisfy the justice of God—which is why it is everlasting. If the fires of hell eventually satisfied God's wrath, hell would come to an end. One drop of the blood of Jesus, however, satisfies the justice of God.

I am acutely and painfully conscious how offensive these lines are to some people. Even if the references to fire are metaphors for conscious pain—which I choose to believe. Do you think I enjoy writing this? I do not. But punishment in hell is not my idea. The German philosopher Ludwig Feuerbach said that God is nothing but man's projection upon the backdrop of the universe.[2] Really? Given that logic, what intelligent human being would have projected hell on the backdrop of the universe as the way God punishes sin? Or sending His Son to die on a cross? No man or woman would have imagined such things.

Hell is God's idea, not mine. Am I to delete the teaching of eternal punishment from my theology because I don't understand it? Or because I don't like it? We are "Christ's ambassadors," says Paul (2 Cor. 5:20). My role is like that of an ambassador. An ambassador defends his government's position even if he does not understand it. I choose to defend the teaching of Scripture because that is my heavenly Father's position. Moreover, it is Jesus who taught it and had the most to say about it.

The teaching of hell and the death of Jesus are inseparably connected. Paul uses a word that means *to turn God's wrath away* when it comes to the blood of Jesus. It is called *propitiation*, a translation from the Greek word *hilasterion*. Paul says that it is the person of Jesus Christ "whom God put forward as a *propitiation by his* blood, to be received by faith" (Rom. 3:25, ESV, emphasis added). *Hilasterion—propitiation*—means "turning God's wrath away." That is what the blood of Jesus does *for God*. We were under the wrath of God. But no more, now that Jesus has died for us—and we believed on Him. This means that Christ's very blood that was shed on the cross keeps you and me from the eternal punishment of God. That blood cried out for justice—and got it. Christ's blood ensures that I will not be punished in hell.

It seems to me also that there has been an ever-increasing trend to destigmatize the gospel, that is, to make it less offensive. One way this is done is by taking the teaching of eternal punishment out of the picture. The other is by removing the idea of *turning God's wrath away* from us when it comes to the atonement of Christ. I am trying to show how these two go together.

This, then, is why people need to be saved.

Many people know the words to the first verse of John Newton's best-known hymn:

> Amazing grace! How sweet the sound
> That saved a wretch like me!
> I once was lost but now am found;
> Was blind, but now I see.

But do you know the second verse?

> 'Twas grace that taught my heart to fear,
> And grace my fears relieved;
> How precious did that grace appear
> The hour I first believed!"[3]

John Newton has thus expressed what drove him to Christ, namely, the fear of the wrath of God. He also was mirroring the historic gospel of Christ in these lines as he does in all his hymns. Until recent times this concept of the gospel was an assumption among most churches. I don't mean to be unfair, but do you honestly believe that preaching generally nowadays instills fear in people that would motivate them to seek God? And yet the earliest message of the New Testament was to "flee" from the coming wrath (Matt. 3:7). Why flee? Because it is so unthinkably horrible.

FOUR IMPORTANT WORDS

There are at least four words we all need for our theological vocabulary.

1. *Propitiation,* which is the best translation of *hilasterion.* As I said, it means turning God's wrath away from us. It is used in Hebrews 9:5, translated "mercy seat" (ESV) and "atonement cover." Jesus Christ is the "propitiation for our sins" (1 John 2:2, ESV) or "atoning sacrifice." I repeat: propitiation refers to *what the blood does for God.* Sadly some people are not interested in what the blood does for God; they only care about what the blood does for us. But our sin has offended God, and He needs to be appeased. The ancient animal sacrifices with their shedding of blood pointed beyond themselves to the cross of Jesus Christ, showing the seriousness of sin and the justice of God. This is precisely why Jesus is called the Lamb of God and Passover Lamb (John 1:29; 1 Cor. 5:7).

2. *Expiation.* Some translate *hilasterion* as expiation. Whereas propitiation refers to what Christ's blood does for God, expiation refers to what the blood does for us—it takes our guilt away, washing away our sins. *Hilasterion* actually refers to both. The

blood of Christ turns God's wrath away *and* takes away our guilt; it guarantees that God's justice is satisfied while it also washes away our sins.

When you realize that the teaching of the blood of Christ is brought in with reference to God's wrath, it makes sense that we use the word *propitiation*. Don't be ashamed of this word; don't forget its meaning.

3. *Satisfaction.* Charles Spurgeon said that there is no gospel apart from these two words: satisfaction and substitution. *Satisfaction* refers to the fact that God's justice is fully appeased by Jesus's death. "Out of the anguish of his soul he shall see and be satisfied" (Isa. 53:11, ESV).

4. *Substitution.* Jesus Christ was our substitute in two ways: His life and His death. He fulfilled the Law for us, believed perfectly for us, and was even baptized for us (Matt. 3:15). He also died for us, taking our place; we are the ones who deserve the punishment, but Jesus was punished for us when He died on the cross. Our sins were transferred to Him as though He were guilty. "The LORD has laid on him the iniquity of us all" (Isa. 53:6). His righteousness was also transferred to us—declaring us innocent; but it—to say it one more time—is applied to us on the condition of our faith. "For our sake he made him to be sin who knew no sin, so that in him we might become the righteousness of God" (2 Cor. 5:21, ESV).

If you say to me that what I have written is difficult to take in, I reply: it ain't over till it's over. I have no doubt that God will explain things clearly to us one day. Until then let us lower our voices and try to remember that His ways are higher than our ways. "As the heavens are higher than the earth, so are my ways higher than your ways and my thoughts than your thoughts," says the Lord (Isa. 55:9). I choose to believe that. I would go to the stake for what I have written.

ASSURANCE OF SALVATION

However, there is another issue that many Christians are not clear about: the ground of our *assurance* of salvation. The problem is often this. Sincere people who are aware of the New Testament demands for holiness often surmise that sanctification must surely be an attached condition to salvation; they believe that if you are not walking in holiness, you have not been truly saved or are ready for heaven. Some well-meaning people inject a question that puts cold water on the excitement that we are saved by faith: "How do you know you have faith?" Whereas I thought that looking to Christ alone *is* faith, some say that you have no right to claim true faith unless you are *also* keeping the works of the Law, are faithful in church, and are consistently resisting sin and the devil. If this is the way I know I have true faith, I end up looking to myself—not Christ— for assurance. The result: endless introspection and assurance based upon what I do for God.

The consequence of this kind of thinking is that—inevitably— the pure gospel passes behind a cloud; it is reduced to sheer works. The reason is obvious. If you tell people they must prove the validity of their faith by good works, they *naturally* look to their sanctification—not Christ's blood—to be sure they make it to heaven.

I have been shocked in my travels around the world since our retirement to discover how few people really understand the gospel. I preach to evangelicals, charismatics, Reformed, Pentecostals. So many of them in their heart of hearts believe sincerely, sadly, that they get to heaven by trusting what they have done for God, not what God has done for us.

We came to England not for me to be the minister of Westminster Chapel but to do research on the English Puritans at Oxford. The Puritans had been my heroes from the days I began to grasp the gospel, but I was not prepared for what I found when I delved very deeply into their thinking. I became almost completely disillusioned. I will never forget it. One day I was reading the works of Thomas Hooker (1586–1647)—the founder of Connecticut—who was writing about "preparation for faith." He taught that in order to have a claim on the gospel you had to be sanctified first. Your ground for assurance was godliness. I had been reading writing by him, Thomas Shepherd, and others like them for months. They stressed sanctification by works of the Law. It was essentially the way I was brought up in my old denomination. I now wondered why I brought my family to England. These Puritans— following William Perkins—made their case that you have no hope of heaven unless you are keeping the Law of God—all of it, including upholding the Sabbath, revering God's ministers—carrying out "universal obedience" (the whole Law). If those things are in place, *then*—and only then—can you lay hold on the promise of salvation.

But one afternoon I had all I could take. I put my hands on the edge of the table in the old library of the British Museum, then pushed my chair back as I looked heavenward. I did not know whether to explode with anger or to weep. I yearned to know: "Am I to preach this? Is this what I am called to preach? Has my pilgrimage led me to this? Is this why I have brought my family from America to England? Why ever did I leave my old denomination if this is true?"

As it turned out, nearly all of those Puritans I studied died without knowing whether they were saved. The most influential of them was William Perkins. He went to his grave in anguish of soul, not knowing whether he was saved or lost.

Can this utter lack of assurance of salvation be a good thing?

I had studied at the Southern Baptist Theological Seminary in Louisville, Kentucky, when it was almost completely liberal. So many of the students around me graduated not knowing whether they could believe the Bible any more. But by the grace of God thankfully I came out of it a stronger evangelical than when I went in. Likewise at Oxford, I came to study the Puritans but by the grace of God finished with a stronger conviction regarding the gospel than when I began. Reading the writings of men such as William Perkins, Thomas Hooker, and Thomas Shepherd almost wrecked me. But I survived.

I remember speaking to a minister friend who seemed to be preoccupied with ecclesiology (doctrine of the church). Every time we met he switched the conversation to the issue of church government, leadership, and authority—matters I regard as secondary. I asked him: "Would you go to the stake for your ecclesiological beliefs?" He replied, "No." I then suggested: "Start preaching on what you would go to the stake for."

I would go to the stake for the gospel. Why? Because those who rest their eternal destinies upon the blood Jesus shed for them on the cross—not their works—*die well*. Moreover, if it is good enough to die well with, it is good enough to live by.

INHERITANCE—NOT SALVATION—MAY BE LOST

You will ask: What happens to those who don't pursue holiness but have trusted in Christ's blood? I reply: they *forfeit their inheritance* and will have no reward at the judgment seat of Christ. The word *inheritance* can be used interchangeably with *reward, prize, crown* (1 Cor. 9:24–27; Col. 3:24; 2 Tim. 4:8). Some New Testament scholars build a case for "justification by works by faith" (my paraphrase to describe their teaching) partly because of 2 Corinthians 5:10: "For we must all appear before the judgment seat of Christ, so that each one of us may receive what is due us for the things done while in the body, whether good or bad." Some believe that *works* play a vital role in salvation. As a consequence they have departed from the gospel. What these scholars have not apparently seen is that all those who are justified by faith are called to enter into their inheritance; some do, some don't. Those who do, have a reward. The basis for this reward is building a superstructure of gold, silver, and precious gems on the foundation—Christ—as put in 1 Corinthians 3:12. Those who build a superstructure of wood, hay or straw will "suffer loss [of reward] but yet will be saved—even though only as one escaping through the flames" (v. 15; saved "as by fire," KJV). There is not a single passage in the New Testament that warns one of losing their salvation; they *all* refer to losing one's inheritance or reward.

To summarize: works necessarily come in where our inheritance is concerned but not whether we go to heaven. Heaven is a free gift by sheer grace (Eph. 2:8–9).

A final irony: those who best understand the gospel are the

ones who want to live a holy life. They, rather than those who trust their works, will be those who are motivated to holy living. What is holy living? Here's a brief list of what I call holiness: total forgiveness, gratitude, sexual purity, financial support for churches, a heart devoid of bitterness, walking in the Spirit, walking in the light, and living for the glory of God. But there is more: holy living is also caring for the poor, the marginalized, those in chains from trafficking, the tortured, and those in prison. True holy living moreover is done out of thankfulness, not in order to earn one's way. This is true godliness—holiness that is derived from grasping the pure gospel. They therefore live holy lives not because it gives them greater assurance of salvation, but because they have their priorities right. The gospel is what saves; holy living is what leads to a reward at the judgment seat of Christ. Some will have such a reward, some won't. But the latter will be saved if their trust is in the blood of Jesus— what God does for us—not what we do for God.

Here is how I know I will be saved by faith alone in Christ's blood alone: the faithfulness of God. God is faithful. He keeps His Word. He will honor the blood of His Son. "Those who honor me I will honor" (1 Sam. 2:30). This is what instills faith, as Martin Luther put it, so daring that you would stake your life—and death—"on it a thousand times."[4]

> My hope is built on nothing less
> Than Jesus' blood and righteousness.
> I dare not trust the sweetest frame,
> But wholly lean on Jesus's name.[5]
> —EDWARD MOTE (1797–1874)

CHAPTER 12

MY LIFE VERSE

How can ye believe, which receive honour one of another,
and seek not the honour that cometh from God only?
—JOHN 5:44, KJV

You weren't put on earth to be remembered. You
were put here to prepare for eternity.[1]
—RICK WARREN

I T WAS THROUGH the influence of Dr. Billy Ball, one of my earliest mentors, that John 5:44 got my attention. Billy happened to be in Nashville, Tennessee, on the same day I experienced the baptism, or sealing, of the Holy Spirit—October 31, 1955. He was then the associate pastor of my old Nazarene church in Ashland, Kentucky, so it was unusual that he would be in Nashville. What happened to me that day had already happened to him years before; he was one of the few people who would truly understand what had occurred. His impact on me was exceeded only by the influence of Dr. Martyn Lloyd-Jones some twenty years later.

Billy Ball and I came out of the Church of the Nazarene at about the same time, although for different reasons. His soteriology remained the same while I had become a Calvinist. One of the things I remember most about him, however, was the way he kept referring to John 5:44—until it gripped me to no end: "How can ye believe, which receive honour one of another, and seek not the honour that cometh from God only?" This is the way the King James Version reads. Most modern versions change "God only" to "the only God." Either is accurate, but the King James Version, in this case it seems to me, puts the weight on seeking the praise from God *alone* and not people. Whatever, that is the way I was spoon fed this verse by Billy Ball from 1955 onward.

As I have never got over the gospel, so too have I never been able to dismiss John 5:44. It is truly my life verse. I often sign Romans 8:28—to which I refer below—to my name when closing a letter or signing a book. But I have sought to be governed by John 5:44. Not that I have faithfully lived it. If only. I wish. But it has always come back to me—haunting me, leading me, encouraging me, warning me, and showing me the path to peace and hopefully keeping me on the right track to the very receiving of the *actual* praise that comes from God alone. I have always wanted to write a book on this verse. But for now I want to show briefly what I think this verse means.

Why the Jews of Jesus's Day
Missed Their Messiah

First, it is a question that Jesus put to certain Pharisees. These certainly did not believe He was the true Messiah. It is as though Jesus says to them in so many words, "Surprise, surprise—so you don't believe in Me? How *could* you believe?" He is virtually saying to them, "You aren't able to believe in Me." Reason: being enslaved to the horrible habit of approval addiction militated against the possibility of true faith. To put it another way, had those Jews to whom the New Testament refers been zealous for the honor and praise that comes from God and not people, they would not have missed their Messiah. But seeking the honor that comes from the one true God was a perspective that was not even on their radar screen. It did not enter their minds! Consequently they missed the greatest promise Israel was ever offered. I like the way the *New International Reader's Version* puts it: Jesus said people like this "do not seek" to obtain the praise that comes from the only God. They didn't even *try*. It was apparently not a part of the way they were trained. And yet that shows how far Judaism generally had departed from God by the time God sent His Son into the world.

I am relieved, I must say, that Jesus inserted the words "seek"— or to suggest that they at least *make an effort*—to obtain the praise of the only God. I am convinced that we aren't *ever* able to be utterly, totally, and without reservation captivated by the praise of God alone so that we don't even enjoy people's praise too. There is something about our sinful minds that still aspire to have the approval and praise of people. I don't think we can ever get over that. I know I haven't. But mercifully Jesus said we can *seek, want, aspire to have,* or *make an effort to receive* the praise of only God—or of God only.

It is like perfect faith. Only Jesus had it. I find myself uttering the words to the Lord, "I do believe; help me overcome my unbelief" (Mark 9:24). So too with the desire to have only God's praise. I know that I want it. I seek it. I do make an effort. I won't give up. But there is that carnal propensity deep inside me that makes me want to look over my shoulder to see if my friends—and enemies—take note of my efforts.

Take, for example, when I preach, it is a temptation I face—no matter how well or how poorly I feel I have done when finishing a sermon. This may surprise you, but I have this need to know how well I did. I will never forget preaching for the Easter People many years ago in Bournemouth, England. I thought I did OK. But I wasn't sure. Would somebody please tell me? But I must not hint to anyone that I am so insecure that I reveal that I am looking for their feedback. It was painful. Normally I would want to head back to London as quickly as possible once the service is over. But I hung around. No one said a word. I headed on back to London, driving the next two hours fearing I had preached poorly. The only plus for me (if I dare put it that way) in all this is that I managed not to hint for anybody's comment. So, yes, I was making an effort. But what is so obvious is that I wasn't content to say, "Lord, I don't care what they think. What do You think?" The desire to get some positive word from someone there was so strong. It was a dead giveaway that what people thought meant too much to me.

WE ARE VULNERABLE TO SELF-RIGHTEOUSNESS

But there is another elephant in the room. One can get very self-righteous about John 5:44. Would I show greater honor to God if I left this chapter out of this book entirely and quietly sought to live this way—and never reveal to the reader that this is the way I aspire to be governed? I could *boast that I am seeking the praise of God only.* But I tell myself that Paul's life verse might have been Exodus 33:13 ("teach me your ways") since his ultimate ambition was "to know Christ" (Phil. 3:10). Paul expressed his supreme wish openly.

So I have sought to come clean; seeking the praise of God is absolutely *the best possible pursuit in this world.* And yet it is like revealing your prayer life. Do I tell you to set an example? Or keep it quiet? I think that maybe we are all better off to know that the Martin Luthers and John Wesleys of this world sought to pray two hours a day. I know for a fact that their examples—and others like them—have inspired me to be a man of prayer over the years. There is no doubt about that. That principle would be my rationale for telling you my most profound wish to receive—somehow—the praise of God *alone.*

Second, this verse implies that you and I forfeit what could have been *ours*—His very praise—when we don't seek the honor that comes from God and not people. The praise that comes from God is absolutely the greatest blessing a person can have not only on planet Earth but also at the judgment seat of Christ. Jesus does not say *when* we receive God's praise. Or what it is. It could come here on the earth. It will certainly come when we stand before God if we have pursued His glory here below. So for some reason Jesus does not say exactly what this praise would be like. But whatever it is, I want it. I want it more than

I want anything in the world. It couldn't get better than this—to have praise, glory, and honor directly from God when you choose His approval above that of friends or enemies.

The Pharisees described in the New Testament were always looking over their shoulders when they did what they did. Their *piety*—praying, fasting, giving—was done only "for people to see" (Matt. 23:5). It is what they lived for. Compliments. Adulation. Respect. Importance. Prestige. That which inflated their egos. Moreover, they feared the consequence of going against the status quo. Being put out of the synagogue was a consequence of believing in Jesus. So the solution was simple: don't believe in Jesus. This is why Nicodemus came to Jesus "at night" (John 3:2) when there was no illumination to show who he was or where he was going. To approach Jesus by day would be too risky. He too feared his fellow Jews—that is, for a good while.

My mentor Rolfe Barnard led me to see how Jonathan Edwards taught us that the task of every generation is to discover in which direction the sovereign Redeemer is moving, then move in that direction. I have been so thankful for Rolfe driving this home to me. Many people miss—or choose to miss—the authentic work of God before their eyes because they fear what people will say. Whether affirming the Welsh revival—which was risky for some, or speaking in tongues—which challenges one's pride, some people are afraid to stand alone. John 5:44 is what should motivate a person to stand alone. And not fear what friends or enemies will say.

The honor of God is worth it. The reward is incalculable. Greater than we can conceive.

But too many people, I fear, come short of even seeking it.

Third, does seeking the honor that comes from the only

true God mean that you must never have the honor of people? Probably not. God may be pleased to give you such favor. But He will grant such blessing only if your *goal* is His honor and not the praise of men. For all I know, *part* of the praise that comes from God alone *is* the favor people may want to bestow on you. This possibility is implicit in Peter's words: "Humble yourselves, therefore, under God's mighty hand, that he may lift you up in due time" (1 Pet. 5:6). In other words, God will allow people's praise if it is not what we seek. The question is whether we can be trusted with people's praise and approval. If that is what we live for, we absolutely kiss good-bye the honor that God would have given us. That is my take on John 5:44.

THE REWARD AT THE JUDGMENT SEAT OF CHRIST IS WORTH WAITING FOR

I have a theory about the way in which the rewards will be handed out at the judgment seat of Christ. My theory is, the greater the praise below, the less at the judgment seat of Christ; the less the recognition below, the greater the reward at the judgment seat of Christ.

Behind this verse is the jealousy of God. This may be a bad quality when it comes to the way you and I must conduct our lives. But it is different with God. He is quite up front about it. As we saw near the beginning of this book, God did not choose to *be* a certain way; He did not make Himself a certain way. He is what and who He is. Like it or not, He is a jealous God. His "name is Jealous" (Exod. 34:14). He will not tolerate competition, as when we want it both ways—seeking His praise and others' praise too. So if you and I seek to live under the principle of John 5:44, it means we must make a deliberate, conscious, and no-turning-back choice to seek His sole approval, and make every effort not to look over our shoulders to see who is watching us.

Finally, what motivates me to seek the honor that comes from God only is that He is faithful. He *will* honor us with His praise. He may hide His face from us here below. He may let us be criticized. We may lose friends. Some suffer—even die for their faith. Martyrdom is possibly the ultimate way we receive the honor that comes from God only. This is why some early Christians literally coveted the chance to be burned at the stake. One could therefore apply this verse in a misleading manner. My job is to covet His honor by following Him and trying to refuse to take compliments seriously. Charles Spurgeon said, "I looked to Christ and the Dove flew in. I looked to the Dove and He disappeared." We must not focus on the reward that might come—or speculate what it would be like. Even if you sense that God is rewarding you with His praise, refuse to dwell on it lest you take yourself too seriously—the problem we all inevitably face. Or the Dove will disappear.

Have you honestly and conscientiously sought after the honor of God but feel it has not been worthwhile? Don't stop making the effort. His praise is worth seeking—and worth waiting for.

CHAPTER 13

VINDICATION

I know that you can do all things; no
plan of yours can be thwarted.
—JOB 42:2

The greatest freedom is having nothing to prove.
—PETE CANTRELL

VINDICATION MEANS TO have your name cleared. It means to be exonerated from a false accusation, to be absolved from blame. It can mean that your reputation is restored, that your integrity and judgment are extolled by the same people who sincerely thought you had been unwise or untruthful. "Commit your way to the LORD; trust in him and he will do this: He will make your righteous reward shine like the dawn, the vindication like the noonday sun" (Ps. 37:5–6).

Do you know what it is to yearn for having your name cleared more than you want anything in the whole world?

In this chapter I will explain why vindication is God's prerogative, and how foolish it can be for us to defend ourselves—no matter how great the temptation. I want to share with you why this issue became important to me and what I have learned about vindication over the years. Events almost sixty years ago led to my grasping this tremendous issue. I hope to show why keeping quiet when falsely accused can be your best way forward.

My first introduction to this vast subject began in March 1956. I prayed a prayer that perhaps I should not have. I had just heard a sermon by Dr. Hugh C. Benner, general superintendent of the Church of the Nazarene, based upon Philippians 2:5–8 (KJV):

> Let this mind be in you, which was also in Christ Jesus: who, being in the form of God, thought it not robbery to be equal with God: but made himself of no reputation, and took upon him the form of a servant, and was made in the likeness of men: and being found in fashion of a man, he humbled himself, and became obedient unto death, even the death of the cross.

Dr. Benner stressed that Jesus had become the lowest possible shame and that we too must have the mind of Christ and therefore be willing to be the lowest possible shame for God's glory. His sermon was so effective that I went immediately to my knees and prayed: "Lord, make me the lowest possible shame for Your glory." Rightly or wrongly I prayed that prayer. I had no earthly idea how that prayer could possibly be answered, for at the time I was on top of the world—a student at Trevecca, pastor of a Nazarene church in Palmer, Tennessee, a promising young preacher in my old denomination, and certainly the pride and joy of my father and grandmother who, a year before, bought me a brand-new Chevrolet to drive to Palmer on weekends.

The following month—April 1956—a series of rather strange and controversial things took place in my old church in Ashland, Kentucky. Billy Ball became involved in these and was suddenly asked to resign as associate pastor. My father wrote me an urgent letter, telling me in no uncertain terms that I must have nothing to do with Billy Ball; I was not to phone him, write him, or see him again. As I read his letter my heart sank. But in that very moment I was given an immediate and direct witness from the Holy Spirit—a clear word from God—to stand with Billy Ball. I was immediately prompted by the Spirit to turn to Philippians 1:12 (NKJV), having no idea what it said: "But I want you to know, brethren, that the things which happened to me have actually turned out for the furtherance of the gospel." I knew without any doubt that God was behind whatever Billy was involved in, but that this would mean breaking with my dad, something I never had done before. That word was so powerful that it held me firm for a long period of time—over twenty years of suffering my father's disapproval.

Parallel with the events at Ashland was my own theological development—an aberration from the theology of my old denomination. Entirely from reading the Bible but not without such revelation by the Holy Spirit, I came to embrace the doctrine of election and the eternal security of the believer. This meant that there would be *two* things to upset my family—my siding with Billy Ball and embracing Calvinism.

The following July my dad accused me of breaking with God. My grandmother took the car back. They meant well. These were godly people. And yet I was called a "disgrace" and "shame" by some of those closest to me. I realized my prayer back in March was answered. The question is, were these events an answer to my ill-posed prayer? Or was I led to pray that way to prepare me for the pain and long haul of being rejected by my father?

Earnest Wish for Vindication

I knew one thing for sure: I wanted vindication more than anything in the world—for something to happen that would convince my dad that I had not broken with God but that I was doing the Father's will. As it happened, vindication would be a long way off. That said, I foolishly did my best to clear my name in those days, defending myself and saying other things that would possibly make me look good in my dad's eyes. Nothing worked. Vindication was delayed for a very long time.

Have you slipped into the trap of wanting to clear your own name and prove that you are in the right? That was my error for so many years.

It has taken me a long time to see for myself what is clearly outlined in Scripture when it comes to vindication: one must not deprive God of doing what is one of the things He does best—to clear one's name. He loves to do this. *But by Himself.* He is the expert! Indeed, but only when *He* does it without our help—and in His time. "'It is mine to avenge; I will repay,' says the Lord" (Rom. 12:19). The worst thing you can do is to elbow in on His territory—and try to help Him! Things will only get worse! That is what I have learned. One might even say I have learned by foolishly trying to vindicate myself. I certainly learned a lot in those days by direct revelation, as I just mentioned. But God allowed me to carry on foolishly in those days, trying to clear my name.

My friend Pete Cantrell has taught me many things. He taught me the temperamental differences between a pigeon and a dove, as I write about in my book *Sensitivity of the Spirit*. But perhaps Pete's greatest observation is that the greatest liberty is having nothing to prove. That means the Holy Spirit sustains a person by Himself; one therefore feels no need to prove anything to anybody!

I only wish I had had this insight in those difficult days in 1956.

My counsel to you: wait on the Lord. He will come through in His time. Have you given up hope? "It ain't over till it's over." "Be still before the LORD and wait patiently for him; do not fret when men succeed in their ways, when they carry out their wicked schemes" (Ps. 37:7).

My initial wish for vindication was merely to have my dad see that I didn't have it wrong. But those were kindergarten days! I could not have known that I was being trained for heavier stuff— to keep quiet when accused of other things down the road! I waited twenty-two years for what I longed for in 1956. As the train was coming into London's King Cross Station in 1978, my father looked at me and said, "Son, I am proud of you. You were right, and I was wrong." That is enough to convince me to wait and stop trying to prove oneself.

Perhaps your particular need for vindication relates to something altogether different from the kind I had needed. The desire for being absolved from an unfair accusation can range from the need for public vindication to something most private—even in your marriage, just between you and your spouse. It can be what you want with family, friends, or foes. In any case or at any level the principle is the same: let God do it. Stay quiet. If you know that God has been with you, you have nothing to prove. But, by the way, don't go around shouting, "I have nothing to prove"— or you could be protesting too much and be trying to prove that you have nothing to prove! If indeed you have nothing to prove, shut up!

What then is the next step forward if it is vindication you want?

GOD AND JESUS

Has it ever crossed your mind that God the Father is the most unvindicated person in the universe? He is the very One people blame the most for all the evil and suffering in the world. The first question people usually ask when you talk to them about Jesus Christ is, "Why is there suffering in the world?" The assumption is that if there is a God who is merciful and all-powerful that He would immediately stop all evil and suffering. What is more, people feel totally at ease in not believing in God; they believe He has a lot to answer for and that they are *entitled* to disbelieve in His existence until He answers their questions.

Have you ever wondered why God does not vindicate Himself when He could surely do so? Why does not God clear His name *now*—if He wants me to believe He exists? For example, the particular Jews to whom the New Testament refers apparently felt completely justified in crucifying Jesus. After all, according to Isaiah, these Jews—at least some of them—considered Him "stricken by him [God]." This means that some believed God Himself was punishing Jesus for claiming to be the Son of God (Isa. 53:4). Certain leaders of the Jews may have assumed that if Jesus were truly the Son of God as He claimed, then God

Himself would come to Jesus's rescue either enabling Him to come down from the cross or by striking His accusers dead. But when they seemed to get away with crucifying Him, they possibly felt all the more convinced they were right to feel as they did and do to Him what they did.

However, while these things were said about those Jews who demanded the crucifixion of Jesus, never forget that not all Jews felt this way. Do not judge Jews generally by calling them Christ killers. The anti-Semitism that has had a long history in some Christian quarters is not pleasing to God. Also, not all in the Sanhedrin agreed to Jesus's crucifixion. Jesus's disciples were Jews. Those who shouted "Hosanna" on Palm Sunday were Jews. The converts on the Day of Pentecost were Jews. The gospel was to the Jew "first" in Paul's day and remains this way (Rom. 1:16).

GOD WILL CLEAR HIS NAME ONE DAY

What is meant by God *clearing* His name? Answer: because countless millions believe He has a lot to answer for—allowing evil in the world when He could stop it in a second, His name is under a cloud. As I said, He is the most unvindicated person in the universe. Clearing His name means that one day He will vindicate Himself. What is more, He will do it in such a manner that *every mouth will be stopped and be totally convinced of God's integrity and justice.*

In a word, God will one day clear His name. On the last day. Count on it. In the meantime He is accused of all the troubles in the world. Consider this: God has made the claim that *everything is put under man's feet.* But is this so? It is written:

> You have made them [man] a little lower than the angels
> and crowned them with glory and honor. You made them

rulers over the works of your hands; you put everything under their feet.

—Psalm 8:5–6

The writer of Hebrews took note of this verse. "In putting everything under them, God left nothing that is not subject to them" (Heb. 2:8). Really? Are we supposed to believe this? Are you and I supposed to believe that evil and suffering—famines, earthquakes, injustices, disease, war and poverty—are put under our feet?

But the writer then adds: "Yet at present we do not see everything subject to them" (Heb. 2:8).

Quite. We certainly *don't* see everything subject to man! So what do you suppose the writer of Hebrews says next? *"But we do see Jesus."* Yes. Does this surprise you? We indeed *don't* see everything subject to us, "but we do see Jesus, who was made lower than the angels for a little while, now crowned with glory and honor because he suffered death, so that by the grace of God he might taste death for everyone" (v. 9).

Here's the point: when you have been falsely accused, when you see evil around you and when injustice prevails in the world God made, look at Jesus. He came to this earth Himself and suffered all the evil and injustice that we creatures experience. This was done partly to let the world know that God Himself is fully aware of what people think and say about Him and what is going on.

Entering Into Jesus's Sufferings

In a word: What are you and I to do when we observe that the things promised by God have not been carried out yet? Answer:

"We see Jesus." We quickly look at Jesus. Jesus's life and death mirror the delayed vindication of God. Jesus did nothing wrong. He never sinned. He did not get a fair trial. Pilate could find no fault in him but gave into the people's demand for Jesus's crucifixion for political reasons. The crucifixion was carried out "with the help of wicked men," said Peter. And yet this was done by "God's deliberate plan and foreknowledge" (Acts 2:23).

It was part of God's plan that His Son be unvindicated, just as the Father remains unvindicated to this very day. It was part of God's purpose.

The God of the Bible is a God of *purpose*. Jesus was crucified by God's set "purpose" ("determinate counsel"—KJV: Greek *orismene boule*—determined, predestined counsel). The crucifixion of Jesus was not an accident. It did not happen because things went wrong. The opposite is true: everything went according to plan! The verse I often put alongside my signature is Romans 8:28: "And we know that all things work together for good to them that love God, to them who are the called according to his *purpose*" (KJV, emphasis added). Those who are called—*saved*—are a part of His eternal purpose. In the same way that the crucifixion was no accident, so too our being converted! God calls us on purpose! The word *purpose* comes from the Greek *prosthesis*. It is used twelve times in the New Testament. It means, "to prefer or place before." It is what is done with intent; it is the opposite of accident.

Here are some examples of how this word is used:

> Yet, before the twins were born or had done anything good or bad—in order that God's *purpose* in election might stand...
>
> —ROMANS 9:11, EMPHASIS ADDED

In him we were also chosen, having been predestined according to the *plan* of him who works out everything in conformity with the purpose of his will.
—EPHESIANS 1:11, EMPHASIS ADDED

According to his eternal *purpose* that he accomplished in Christ Jesus our Lord.
—EPHESIANS 3:11, EMPHASIS ADDED

He has saved us and called us to a holy life—not because of anything we have done but because of his own *purpose* and grace.
—2 TIMOTHY 1:9, EMPHASIS ADDED

Therefore what wicked men did to Jesus, then, was carried out by God according to His eternal plan and purpose.

But there is more. The absence of vindication was part of the package.

God wanted you and me to know what it was like for Jesus to suffer and be blamed for injustice—even charged with blasphemy! When the council of elders asked Jesus, "'Are you then the Son of God?' He replied, 'You say that I am.' Then they said, 'Why do we need any more testimony? We have heard it from his own lips?'" (Luke 22:70–71). This was "blasphemy" and "worthy of death," the high priest said (Matt. 26:65–66).

JESUS'S VINDICATION

But here is the notable thing. After Jesus was raised from the dead, He appeared only to those who believed in Him previously. He showed Himself to believers, not to His accusers. Had God wanted to vindicate Jesus openly He might have gone straight to the house of the high priest on Easter morning or to

Herod's palace. Jesus might have knocked on Pilate's door and said, "Surprise!" But no.

Jesus's vindication before the world was delayed. He appeared to Mary Magdalene. He appeared to Peter. He appeared to the eleven. He appeared to "more than five hundred of the brothers and sisters at the same time" (1 Cor. 15:6). Moreover, the Holy Spirit fell on one hundred twenty believers who had tarried in Jerusalem as Jesus instructed them (Luke 24:49). But vindication stayed within the family.

Paul says that Jesus was "vindicated by the Spirit" (1 Tim. 3:16). This means two things: vindication was internal for Him and internal for us. The external vindication is delayed until the day He returns to the earth and "every eye will see him" (Rev. 1:7). Why is Jesus's vindication internal—by the Spirit? First, Jesus got His approval when He was on earth from within—from the Father by the Holy Spirit—not from people. He did not look to His disciples for authentication. Can you imagine Jesus calling Peter or John to one side and asking them, "What did you think of my sermon on the mount?" "Did you think I handled the Pharisees well?"

Second, it is you and I who vindicate Jesus—by the Holy Spirit. It is we who affirm (1) who He is—the God-man, (2) why He died—to satisfy God's justice, and (3) where He is—at the right hand of God. Only believers know this! Try telling the world that Jesus the God-man was raised from the dead after dying on the cross—then ascending to heaven to the right hand of God the Father. And yet that is where Jesus is now. But who believes this? Only those who have been quickened by the Holy Spirit. This then is what is meant by Jesus's vindication by the Spirit.

The external vindication of Jesus awaits His Second Coming.

This is when He will come to judge the living and dead. Every knee shall bow and every tongue confess that Jesus Christ is Lord to the glory of God the Father (Phil. 2:10–11). You and I do it now—by the Holy Spirit. But one day everybody will do it—not because they are saved but because they will be compelled to.

In the meantime we are to learn that the only vindication that is promised below is internal—like that of Jesus. This comes by seeking the honor that comes from the only God (John 5:44). There is nothing more sublime than the inner testimony of the Holy Spirit. The Spirit tells us that we are approved by God. It doesn't get better than that.

But is it *external* vindication that you want? I can understand that. It is the most natural desire in the world—to want people who have doubted you to see for themselves that you had got it right.

JOB

Almost certainly nobody in the Old Testament suffered as Job did. External vindication is exactly what Job wanted. He went through extreme suffering. It began when Job—who was both very godly and very wealthy—suddenly received terribly bad news. Some people called Sabeans attacked and carried off Job's oxen and donkeys and put his servants to the sword. At the same time fire from the sky burned up Job's sheep and servants. Not only that, but the Chaldeans also formed raiding parties and swept down on Job's camels and carried them off while putting the servants to the sword. But there was more: a strong wind swept in from the desert and struck his home; it collapsed and killed his sons and daughters (Job 1:16–19).

Job reacted amazingly to the bad news. He said, "'The LORD gave and the LORD has taken away; may the name of the LORD be praised.' In all this, Job did not sin by charging God with wrongdoing" (Job 1:21–22).

So far, so good. A new wave of suffering came to Job. He was afflicted with painful sores from the soles of his feet to the top of his head. He took a piece of broken pottery and scraped himself with it as he sat among ashes. "His wife said to him, 'Are you still maintaining your integrity? Curse God and die!'" Job rebuked his wife for speaking as she did. "'You are talking like a foolish woman. Shall we accept good from God, and not trouble?' In all this, Job did not sin in what he said" (Job 2:7–10).

Again, so far, so good. But at this stage a different kind of suffering for Job emerged. He had three friends who observed his suffering. They could hardly recognize him. They began to weep aloud, tearing their robes and sprinkling dust on their heads. They said nothing to him at first. But before long they began to speak to Job and accused him of sin in his life, otherwise this evil would not have come upon him. That was the prevailing theology of Job's day: it was generally assumed that suffering was due to sin.

The truth was, Job had *not* sinned. The truth was, he truly *was* "blameless and upright; he feared God and shunned evil" (Job 1:1). But the three men—called "friends"—ruthlessly attacked Job, accusing him day and night of having some secret sin. Nothing he could say convinced them that he was innocent.

It is one thing for Job to be put through the suffering—losing his family, the great financial loss he was put through plus intense physical pain—but to be accused of bringing this on by his own sin was more than he could cope with. Although Job had been "blameless" there was nonetheless a spiritual dimension he had not thought about—and probably never considered: his self-righteousness. He eventually lost his temper, protested his innocence to such a ridiculous degree that he became obnoxious—and was clearly in a bad, even pathetic, spiritual state. He ended up sinning after all. Wouldn't we all?

My point is this. Job so craved external vindication in order that these horrible men would somehow see that there was no secret sin that caused all his suffering. When you are falsely accused, when you have not done what people think you have done, when you have maintained integrity and when your deepest motive was to honor God alone, the temptation is to want your name to be cleared in the eyes of people. You are afraid that justice will not be done, that unfairness will prevail. Job completely lost it and caused his "friends" to feel totally vindicated in their accusations.

WHILE WE WAIT WE CAN LEARN A LOT

There are some subsidiary principles, however, that are encouraging. First, we can learn *a lot* while we are waiting for vindication. The yearning for external vindication is what drives us to our knees. We may not realize it at the time, but it is when we learn more of God's *ways*. This is invaluable knowledge. Second, the longer we wait the sweeter vindication will be. If one is vindicated in the short run—that is, soon after your integrity was called into question—the chances are that you won't fully appreciate the vindication. But when it is postponed, you are learning God's ways and you will find the outcome sweeter than honey. Third, the greater the grief the higher the level of pleasure there will be when God steps in to clear your name. He lets us suffer for so long, but part of the reason for the suffering is that we can have greater joy for having had to wait. What God envisages for you is worth waiting for. "It ain't over till it's over." When it is *over* you will have no complaints against God for His strategy in letting you wait.

But there is still a greater truth to be grasped: God Himself had permitted the entire ordeal. Yes, God allowed Satan to instigate the whole scenario of Job's suffering. Nothing takes God by surprise. God had said to Satan, "Have you considered my servant Job? There is no one on earth like him; he is blameless and upright, a man who fears God and shuns evil" (Job 1:8). So God allowed what followed. However, the devil was given permission to proceed so far and no further; Satan was not permitted to take Job's life (Job 2:6).

Job needed to learn that although he was outwardly blameless and truly feared the Lord, he was still a sinner! He did not realize how much God hates self-righteousness. The problem that the Pharisees had with Jesus's teaching was that they saw themselves as sinless as long as they were outwardly moral. The righteousness that surpassed that of the Pharisees was an *inner* righteousness—where there was an absence of hate and lust. So when God stepped in and answered Job out of the storm, Job said: "I despise myself and repent in dust and ashes" (Job 42:6).

JOB'S GREATEST LESSON

But the greatest lesson of all for Job was to learn a most thrilling, peace inducing truth: "I know that you can do all things; no purpose of yours can be thwarted" (Job 42:2). Knowing that no plan of God can be thwarted is far greater knowledge than experiencing external vindication. For when you realize that

God's plan for you will not be aborted—despite your sinfulness and straying—you have inner peace and joy. When Job saw that underneath his wretchedness were God's everlasting arms, he was set. Yes, he was totally vindicated in the end. He had an external vindication. God even gave Job more than he had in the beginning. But the greatest joy of all was to know how great, powerful, and wonderful God is.

May I ask you: have you discovered what Job found out—that no plan of God can be thwarted? This means that nothing can prevent God from succeeding at the end of the day. This is an extraordinary statement. I don't know if this is what Job had always believed, but he certainly believed it in the end! It took the long suffering and God showing up as He did to persuade Job of this truth. Again, it is an amazing statement. Do you believe this—that no plan of God can be thwarted in the end? I would have thought there are two ways by which one would come to this kind of thinking:

1. Intellectually—when you come to this by reason

2. By an immediate and direct witness of the Holy Spirit

I am satisfied that it is the latter that Job experienced. It is one of the most amazing truths one can grasp.

Job's vindication had seemed utterly out of sight. Job and his friends dialogued in what seemed like endless, unprofitable, and pointless exchanges. There was not the slightest hint throughout these harsh dialogues that Job's friends would be compelled to withdraw their accusations. And they never—ever—would have affirmed Job as a man of integrity had not God Himself stepped in. When God stepped in it was *over.* "I am angry with you," God said to these hard, relentless "friends." "You have not spoken the truth about me, as my servant Job has" (Job 42:7). Job had no idea that God would do this. He had been demoralized, hurt, angry, full of himself, and hopeless. But underneath Job was God's eternal love.

IT IS TRUTH RATHER THAN YOU THAT IS VINDICATED

Vindication is not personal, that is, one should not seek vindication because it makes you look good. It is the *truth* that is vindicated. It is not primarily about you. Abraham Lincoln once said that "truth is generally the best vindication against slander."[1] But if you have stood for the truth, you are in a good place. Truth is indeed the best vindication against slander, being misunderstood or false accusation. Just wait.

The apostle Paul suffered from having some of his converts in Corinth turn against him. Imagine pain like this—having the very people you led to Christ turn against you or doubt you. A group of Jews—we call them *Judaizers* today—followed Paul from place to place. Their purpose was to undermine Paul's influence. They told Paul's Gentile converts that they were not being given the whole truth, that they need to be circumcised and get themselves under the Law. The result was that some of Paul's converts in Corinth felt deprived of truth and that Paul had let them down by not telling them they need to be circumcised.

Paul's reply was amazing:

> I care very little if I am judged by you or by any human court; indeed, I do not even judge myself. My conscience is clear, but that does not make me innocent. It is the

Lord who judges me. Therefore judge nothing before the appointed time; wait till the Lord comes. He will bring to light what is hidden in darkness and will expose the motives of the heart. At that time each will receive their praise from God.

—1 Corinthians 4:3–5

It was the truth that mattered. God will vindicate the truth. Those who are on the side of truth will be vindicated. But it is not primarily personal. When Paul says he does not even judge himself he was putting himself under Jesus's teaching that we should not let our right hand know what our left hand is doing (Matt. 6:3). Whereas the original context referred to giving alms to be seen of people, Jesus taught that there is a sense in which we do not even tell ourselves what good we may have done—lest we take ourselves too seriously. This is why Paul could say that he does not even judge himself. Let the Lord decide, and He will in His time. Vindication may be delayed until the Second Coming. But sometimes it comes sooner—when God chooses to step in, as He did with Job.

The main thing is that we *wait*. We do not vindicate ourselves. We wait for God to vindicate the truth.

Vindication Then, Vindication Now

David wanted vindication. On one occasion when David clearly spared King Saul's life, refusing to lay a hand on the king, he nonetheless said to Saul: "May he [God] consider my cause and uphold it; may he vindicate me by delivering me from your hand" (1 Sam. 24:15).

Vindication that comes in the future, then, is external. There is the *then* and the *now*. Then is the future; that is when *all* see the truth. But there is one thing we can all have *now*—the internal testimony of the Spirit. It is what Jesus enjoyed—vindication by the Holy Spirit. Internal vindication. If we are given that immediate witness of the Holy Spirit, it means inexpressible joy. But you won't be allowed to tell others. Nor should you. The moment you tell others you violate the principle of vindication—that it is for the glory of God.

"It ain't over till it's over." The *over* might mean external vindication. Or it could be internal. Either way, how God chooses to bring vindication is worth waiting for.

CHAPTER 14

GOD'S PLAN AND CALLING

Do not conform to the pattern of this world, but be transformed
by the renewing of your mind. Then you will be able to test and
approve what God's will is—his good, pleasing and perfect will.
—ROMANS 12:2

God loves you and offers you a wonderful plan for your life.[1]
—BILL BRIGHT (1921–2003)

W E NOTED EARLIER that Job learned that "no purpose
of yours can be thwarted" (Job 42:2). But is this true of
everyone? It was true for Job. Granted. But what about you? Can
you honestly affirm that no plan of God for you has been thwarted?

Did not Paul aspire to visit Thessalonica? But then said, "Satan
blocked our way" (1 Thess. 2:18; "hindered us," ESV). Whatever

does that mean? If the great apostle Paul can be stopped by Satan, where does that leave you and me?

What about people who wanted to be married? Or have children? What about those called into the ministry but decided later they weren't called after all? What about those whose marriages were nightmares—and sadly (or perhaps happily) came to an end? What went wrong? Can one marry out of God's will?

This chapter is the most difficult in this book to write. I wish I could give simple, short, concrete, encouraging, and totally convincing and complete answers. I cannot. But does that mean we cannot approximate the truth? I hope we can. Mind you, we are bordering on the mystery of prayer, the mystery of evil, and the recondite issue of predestination.

THE CALL TO PREACH

Let's begin with the matter of knowing God's will, or calling, for your life. I choose to begin with the call to preach. This is pretty much up my alley.

"If you can do anything else, do it," the great Charles H. Spurgeon used to counsel people who wanted to go into the preaching ministry. My pastor in Ashland, Kentucky, always said the same thing: "Be sure you are called of God, for the worst thing that can happen is to be in the ministry if God did not call you." I therefore grew up with a fear of going into the ministry and not being called of God to do it. I had a burning desire to preach, but I was afraid it was a natural wish. One of my oldest friends had a rather spectacular call. He heard a voice, "Dale, will you preach." I wanted something like that—perhaps Michael the archangel appearing to me. Michael never came.

I was a student at Trevecca Nazarene College (now University) when a Scottish preacher, Dr. John Sutherland Logan from near Glasgow, visited our campus in November 1954. When I heard him, I declared it was the greatest preaching I had ever heard. Sixty years later I would still say much the same thing about his style. I sought eagerly to get to spend time with Dr. Logan, and managed to have breakfast with him a few times. On the last day before he left Nashville I said to him, "How can I know if I am called to preach."

He replied: "You are."

I said, "But I need to know for sure that I am called."

"You are," he said quite bluntly, repeating it. And guess what? I believed him. For some reason I never doubted it, I never looked back. But what a disappointment to get such an unspectacular call!

Years later when I was a student at Southern Baptist Seminary in Louisville, Kentucky, I had my heart set on working on a research degree in Great Britain. This is because the same Dr. Logan always expressed his wish that I go to Edinburgh, Scotland, to do post-graduate work. He thought I should study under the famed professor T. F. Torrance. So I had every plan to do this. I even drove hundreds of miles to meet Dr. Torrance when he was in America lecturing. I had a meal with Dr. Torrance and corresponded with him often. I let him know that I would be in Britain on a certain day in January 1972 and could come to Edinburgh but only on one particular date. He wrote back that unfortunately he would be too busy to see me at that time. That came as a real downer. This meant I would have extra time in London with nothing to do. I then arranged to see Dr. J. I. Packer and Dr. Martyn Lloyd-Jones. (Can you imagine anything more incredulous than either J. I. Packer or Martyn Lloyd-Jones being anyone's plan B? But they were for a brief moment. My plan B was God's plan A.) I was invited by each of them to come to their homes. I had dinner with Dr. Packer when he was a tutor at Trinity College, Bristol. The following day I had an entire evening with Dr. and Mrs. Lloyd-Jones whom I first met years before at Winona Lake, Indiana. Both of them recommended that I *not* go to Edinburgh but to Oxford and study the English Puritans. What had been a severe disappointment—not getting to go to Edinburgh to study under Torrance—turned out to be the best thing that could have happened to me.

THE PERMISSIVE WILL OF GOD

If I have learned *anything* about the ways of God in my lifetime it is this: God has a purpose in what He allows, *no matter what* it is and however disappointing, whether great or small. I truly believe that whatever happens comes within the scope of the *permissive will of God* and with a hidden purpose He already planned. Nothing ever catches God by surprise. This means that God has a strategic, thought out purpose in allowing things to happen.

I did not say everything that happens is predestined. Some Reformed thinkers might say everything is predestined. I am not saying that. If you ask, "What is the difference between what God *causes* and what He *permits*?," I answer: I don't know. It seems to me we hit a wall. We are confronted with an unknowable point of divine knowledge. We may wish to knock down the wall or somehow get past it and figure it all out. We may be like Moses when he saw the burning bush, who said, "I will go over and see this strange sight—why the bush does not burn up." God interrupted: "Do not come any closer." Instead, "Take off your sandals, for the place where you are standing is holy ground" (Exod. 3:3–5).

The difference between what God predestines and what He permits is holy ground. Take off your shoes. Don't try to figure it out. Even a theological Einstein cannot explain this—believe me.

The nearest you come—in my opinion—to a sense of sanity on this issue is to accept J. I. Packer's use of the word *antinomy*. He told me he got it from Immanuel Kant (1724–1804). It means two parallel truths that are irreconcilable but both true. Dr. Packer suggests that theologically it means parallel principles that *appear to us* irreconcilable but are both true. For example, God has sovereignly chosen His people from the foundation of the world and yet commands us to preach the gospel to every person. These are contradictory. And yet both are true. The problem is most people select one or the other and cannot accept both. But if you can accept both, you are well on your way to theological peace. Don't try to figure it out. Whether it is the Trinity or the truth of Jesus being simultaneously God and man, just believe it!

BE WILLING NOT TO KNOW EVERYTHING

You are not required to believe everything that happens is predestined. Be content with the belief that there are some things predestined and other things that are in God's permissive will.

Be willing not always to know which is which. Relax.

Can you accept this?

Why is the answer to this so important? First, you are too likely to panic or be severely tempted not to believe in God when evil comes your way if you do not believe that God has a purpose in what He allows. The first reaction of many is to conclude, "There is no God," when something horrible takes place—whether it be war, famine, poverty, hurricanes, people born with impediments, or when fiendish crimes are carried out. As I write these lines the world is aghast that reporters in the Middle East have been beheaded by an Islamic terrorist. "How can there be a God when things like this exist?" is a common question when such awful things occur. The only healing antidote in a time like this is an unswerving, robust belief that God is a God of purpose.

Close to this line of thinking is a belief in the existence of the devil. Evil is present in this world. God allowed it. The devil is also very intelligent and very powerful but less powerful and less knowledgeable than God. God is bigger, better, and will win. God is in control, not Satan, although God gives the devil a measure of scope. Accept the fact of Satan and evil and know that God is greater. Believe the Bible and don't assume your mind is superior to simple faith in the Word of God. Don't analyze. Just believe. To paraphrase St. Augustine, "Seek not to understand that you may believe, but believe that you may understand."[2] This became a dominant epistemological axiom in Reformed theology: *faith seeking understanding.*

Believing that God permits things for a purpose does not mean that He causes evil things to happen. You will say: "But if God could have stopped evil but doesn't, does this not mean He caused it?" No. We have no right to come to this conclusion. You will reply: "But what other logical conclusion can we reasonably come to if that is not the case?" I reply: we don't know. You will probably say, "That's not good enough." I can understand your thinking. This is the fork in the road to which we all come. Some opt for atheism; some choose to trust in the integrity of the God of the Bible, vindicate God *now* and then wait for His explanation in heaven. Are you able to do that? If so, you and I are on the same page.

Here's the reality: philosophically or theologically one comes to *an unknowable point* in trying to figure things out. Atheism is, for some, a most attractive option. I call it the easy way out. Or you can listen to the Holy Spirit—Who wrote the Bible using people He raised up—and embark on the most exciting venture that ever was. That venture is a life of faith!

POLAR OPPOSITES: THEODICY VERSUS EXISTENTIALISM

There are two polar opposites when it comes to one's world view of faith: theodicy or existentialism. Theodicy is the belief that God is a God of purpose, that He is in full control of what is going on in the whole universe. This means there is a reason for the bad things He permits, that God allows all things for a reason. A good reason. His reason. A good purpose. His purpose. He is not a God who created the world and then left it to run itself—like an absentee watchmaker. No. He not only *knows* all that is happening but is also consciously upholding all things by the word of His power (Heb. 1:1–3). This is the classic Christian belief, and it is what I believe.

At the other end of the spectrum is existentialism—the idea that we have somehow been *thrown* into our *existence*. We don't know how we got here. We will never know. There is neither rhyme nor reason for things happening as they do. You don't know today, you won't know tomorrow; you will never know. Those are the conclusions of the existentialist. Life is "absurd" said John Paul Satre (1905–1980). Some of his disciples began committing suicide—the logical thing to do, they said, so Satre then climbed down! That said, if there is no God of purpose, then existentialism is the logical choice.

OPEN THEISM—DON'T GO THERE

In between, however, is a growing belief called open theism. One premise of this is that God is enriched by His creation. I will admit that there is something enticing about this line of thought. But beware; it is an angel of light, a way of luring you away from the God of the Bible. If God can be enriched by His creation, it means He is dependent upon His creation to be fulfilled in Himself. The truth is, God is happy in Himself without creating a speck of dust. Creation is what He chose to do. He is not enriched by it, but He is glorified by it. These two are not the same thing. To be enriched suggests there was some degree of impoverishment in the first place. God is not—or ever was—impoverished. He is the everlasting omnipotent and omniscient God. He does things for His glory. This is the God of the Bible. The proponents of open theism are often existentialists and afraid of an omniscient God but still wanting to hold on to a belief in God. But they have to compromise their premises if they accept the God of the Bible. For the God of the open theist is not all powerful, neither is He all knowing. He certainly does not know the future—except by probability, by guessing. So when you pray to a God like this to get His wisdom, he must shout back, "You tell me, I need your help to know what to do next." Moreover, there is no guarantee that such a God will win in the end! With open theism there is no objective hope that God will win in the end; the proponents of this theory only choose to believe He will win in the end. The God of the Bible *will* win in the end—whether we choose to believe it or not.

The book you are now reading is written because the God of the Bible is a God of purpose. There is a reason for things that happen—good or bad. There is never a need to panic. And if you are tempted to come to a hasty conclusion as to why God has allowed this or that in your life, consider this: "It ain't over till it's over." Be willing not to know everything. We used to sing back in the hills of Kentucky, "Someday He'll Make it Plain." I believe that.

These things said, I admit that my deepest and most painful concern is for those who have suffered more than I have and who have had problems I have not had.

For example, I myself can totally agree with Job: nothing can thwart God's plan that is for me. I happen to believe that with all my heart. But I accept there are those who say, "Something went badly wrong in my experience. I prayed, nothing happens. I became a Christian, nothing worked out for me." Some of these were brought up in Christian homes—just as solid and secure as my own, but they have had unthinkably unhappy marriages, loneliness, most painful rejections, poor health, financial problems galore, extreme physical pain, and a feeling there is literally nothing to live for. People like this have suffered far more than I have. These people would not merely say that they were "hindered" by Satan but that the devil has taken over completely. And the more they pray they more confused they get.

What are we to say about people like this? I will answer as I *have* answered people like this by the hundreds. In a word: *not to give up.* It ain't over till it's over.

The God Who loves me loves them as much as He loves me.

And if you have been overwhelmed with problems equal to or worse than what I have described above, I answer: God loves you as much as He loves me.

Yes, God Does Have a Wonderful Plan for Your Life

Dr. Bill Bright founded Campus Crusade many years ago. The opening line in their evangelistic message is: God loves you and offers a wonderful plan for your life. Countless tens of thousands have been won to Christ by this method. But many have also asked, "If God has a wonderful plan for me, what happened to it?"

I want to be as fair as I can with you—should you be somewhat like the one I just described. Would you consider coming back to God—and starting again? Would you consider adopting Romans 12:2 as a way of life: "Do not conform to the pattern of this world, but be transformed by the renewing of your mind"? If you will do this with unfeigned resolution—and not give up, I can guarantee that you will be able to say down the road that (1) you discovered "what God's will is—his good, pleasing and perfect will" (v. 2); and also that (2) "all things" have, after all, worked together for "good" (Rom. 8:28).

Don't try to figure out what happened—or how it got this way. Be willing to start again. Don't look back. Turn to the God of the Bible. Try again. He is there waiting for you and will take over—starting now—and begin causing all that has happened to work together for good.

So whether you were truly called to preach and gave it up, or married one who appeared to be the wrong person, took the horrible job, made a foolish decision, got mixed up with unhelpful people who influenced you, or were let down by what you thought were the very best of people, turn to Jesus Christ. He will accept you. If you are granted repentance, it is a brilliant sign that God is on your case and that, sooner or later, your regrets will be minimal.

God does have a wonderful plan—for the rest of your life.

CHAPTER 15

FINISHING WELL

*I have fought the good fight, I have finished the race, I
have kept the faith. Now there is in store for me the
crown of righteousness, which the Lord, the righteous
Judge, will award to me on that day—and not only to
me, but also to all who have longed for his appearing.*
—2 TIMOTHY 4:7–8

It's not how you start that's important, but how you finish![1]
—JIM GEORGE

I STARTED WELL. I was born into a godly Christian home on
July 13, 1935, in Ashland, Kentucky. God and the church
were first in my parents' lives. My earliest memory of my dad
was seeing him on his knees praying every morning before he

went to work. My earliest memory of my mother was seeing her on her knees praying after dad went to work. I would wait somewhat impatiently for her to finish. I knew she was almost finished when she lifted her hands into the air, worshipping.

Some twenty years later when I was as a student at Trevecca Nazarene College, the Rev. C. B. Cox was a guest preacher there. Other than the preaching of John Logan, his sermon is the only one I can remember in some detail during my time at Trevecca. He took his text from Hebrews 11:5—about Enoch who had this testimony before his translation, that he "pleased God." I was very moved by that sermon. It made me want to go to my dormitory room and kneel and pray. I wrote my dad a letter and told him about it. He told me this story: "Son, when your mother was six months pregnant with you, we happened to attend the Nazarene Church in Indianapolis, Indiana. I was so gripped by the preacher's sermon that I put my hand on your mother's tummy and prayed, 'Lord, let my son [he was obviously hoping for a son] grow up to preach the gospel and preach like this man.' The name of that preacher was C. B. Cox."

Paul: Our Role Model for Finishing Well

The apostle Paul finished well. Any follower of Jesus Christ would want to finish as Paul did. He is the model for all of us. And though no one could match the apostle Paul for greatness, surely we should want to be as faithful as he was. His end is as triumphant and satisfying as it could possibly get. Imagine coming to the close of a life in which you traveled all over the Mediterranean, not as a tourist but as a hated evangelist of the gospel of Jesus Christ, one who suffered persecution nonstop and coped with the loss of reputation in places that meant most to him. One who endured tortuous loneliness, wrote virtually two thirds of the New Testament epistles (which he could not have envisaged at the time), escaped death again and again. He wrote the words "I have finished the race, I have kept the faith" while waiting to be beheaded by the Caesar at any moment.

Yes, Paul should be our model for finishing well. But to what extent can I be the apostle Paul?

What is the cause that some do not finish well?

DISAPPOINTMENT FROM UNREALISTIC AMBITION

Many people feel they have not finished well because their reality fell short of their dream; their achievement in life came short of their expectation when they were young. Sometimes disappointment may be traced to unrealistic goals. This has been a huge problem in my own life—unrealistic goals. I was taught early on to "hitch your wagon to a star," as the American essayist Ralph Waldo Emerson put it. That means aspire to greatness, to aspire to be the greatest of achievers. I chose heroes who were the best—the very best. Joe DiMaggio, the great baseball player for the New York Yankees, was my first hero. In the music world I esteemed and even tried to emulate Arthur Rubinstein, probably the greatest pianist of his generation. My favorite composer has always been Sergei Rachmaninoff whose symphonies and concertos do more for me emotionally than some religious songs. My chief mentor was Dr. Martyn Lloyd-Jones, arguably the greatest preacher—ever.

To put it another way, possibly because of the way I was brought up, I created unrealistic dreams in my mind. I so wanted to be the best at something. But I never was. I never excelled in sports, although I loved playing basketball. I love to fish but was never truly a very good fisherman. I was a mediocre pianist. I wrote a few songs. I introduced some of them to Westminster Chapel! No one asked to have any of them sung again. And as for preaching, I am a pygmy compared to my giant mentor. I have found peace by embracing a different perspective. What does God truly *expect* of us? Does He set unrealistic goals for us? Not at all! We must learn to get our contentment from pleasing God—alone. None of us can match the apostle Paul. There never was another like him. We cannot be St. Athanasius, St. Augustine, Martin Luther, John Calvin, or Jonathan Edwards.

Here is the truth that has saved me: God Himself chooses our inheritance for us (Ps. 47:4)—which includes our calling, ability, anointing, gifts, type of ministry, profile, uniqueness, places of ministry, open doors, closed doors, friends, and enemies. God knows what is best for us and wants what is best for us. Our only responsibility is to be faithful. If we carry out what God has envisioned for us—knowing our limitations—we should feel as fulfilled as the apostle Paul.

An Important Distinction

I want to make a distinction between finishing well generally and finishing well particularly. I would therefore want to make a distinction between:

1. Saved people vis-à-vis lost people

2. Saved people vis-à-vis those Christians who do not seem to finish well

Finishing well generally means being ready to meet God at the time of your death. I am not talking about having been successful in your job or calling. Nor am I talking about how famous you are or whether people praise you for your accomplishments in life. You may have monuments erected in your name. You may have a street named after you. But these accolades do not mean that you finished well. Whoever would want a monument erected in their honor while they are still alive? Or made sure it was carried out after their death? I know two men who made sure this was done—Saul and Absalom. Neither of these men finished well. A *life* that ended well is the only kind of monument we should aspire to. Whether we have truly finished well is ultimately determined by the verdict that will be revealed at the judgment seat of Christ.

It's Not Over Until You Die

Finishing well or not finishing well is determined by your spiritual state when you die.

Jesus told a story about two people who died at about the same time. One was a nameless rich man, the other a beggar named Lazarus. It was the poor man who finished well. There would have been no obituary of his life in the *New York Times*. No one would speak of his great accomplishments at his funeral—if he had a funeral. He had nothing to live for on the earth, but he went to heaven when he died. If you are ready to meet God when you die, you have finished well. On the other hand, the rich man had everything to live for on the earth. He might have been praised in major newspapers when he died. He may well have had an expensive coffin and was extolled for his accomplishments by a clergyman at his elaborate funeral.

But while he was being honored, he was actually in hades, a place of torment. The rich man also had his memory in hades—which would make this place even worse. *Hades* is a word that means "the grave" or "death," but it is also a place where a person could feel pain. This man who had been rich in his lifetime was not able to do anything about his state now that he was in hades. On earth he would have been able to buy his way out of a jam. He would have had influence to make things happen. But not here. Nobody could come to his aid. It was a permanent place of regret and hopelessness. (See Luke 16:19–31.) The rich man did not finish well. A great name in life, yes, but a nameless failure in eternity.

If you want to finish well, imitate the man who went to heaven. First, he had a name—Lazarus. Jesus told us to rejoice that our "names" are written in heaven (Luke 10:20). God calls us by our "name" (Isa. 43:1). Second, Lazarus was a beggar. If you don't become a beggar while you are alive—that is, to plead with God for mercy—you will become a beggar in hades. The rich man was begging for relief from his pain. But it was too late. The rich man did not finish well.

KNOWING YOU ARE SAVED IS THE BEGINNING OF FINISHING WELL

This is what I mean by finishing well generally. It means knowing that you are saved. Therefore by the term *finishing*—in this case—I mean *death*. When it's *over*. Not retirement. Not moving from one job or position to another.

So in this final chapter I am talking about our last breath. It is appointed unto all humankind "to die once" (Heb. 9:27). Everybody will die. Woody Allen is famous for saying, "I'm not afraid to die, I just don't want to be there when it happens."[3] I only dread the possibility of pain before dying. But I want to be there when it happens—and, may it please God, be conscious right to the end. I might well be in pain—who could look forward to that? But I do look forward to the very moment my spirit departs from this mortal body. I fully expect to see Jesus's face the very second I pass away.

Being appointed to die "once" in Hebrews 9:27 is a word we might not notice. It is there on purpose: a reminder that *we only have one life*. This life is *it*. You have one body—the very body you were born with. You have one mind, one soul, one life. There won't be another. You will be conscious beyond the grave, yes. But any teaching that suggests you will have another chance to live in a future life is false. Those who accept the notion that they might do better the next time around—in a future life—are speculating on sheer fantasy at best or accepting satanic teaching at worst.

You therefore finish well in this general sense I have referred to if you are saved when you die. Salvation is by the sheer grace of God; it is His free gift and is received by relying on Christ's blood. Whether you are saved as a child or ten minutes before you die, eternity lasts a long time—forever and ever. To miss heaven is to miss all that ultimately matters; it means to incur God's eternal wrath. Fifty years of being a faithful Christian is no advantage over being saved at the last moment—insofar as where you spend eternity is concerned. The scandal of the gospel is that one can live a respectable moral life and have a good reputation—and not finish well. This is because not to be saved is to finish in the worst possible imaginable state. On the other hand, one may live the worst possible life until the end—then turn to Christ, as the thief on the cross did, and be saved.

A Christian Life Finishing Well

I now refer to the previously mentioned phrase, finishing well particularly. This means saved people vis-à-vis those saved people who do not finish well. John Wesley had a word for his critics: "Our people die well."[4] The early Methodists could not have had a better commendation than that.

I therefore now deal with the issue of a Christian who finishes well. You will possibly ask: Don't all Christians finish well? Sadly, no. There have even been Christian leaders who have not finished well. This includes those who had moral failures. It may include those who did not plan ahead and left their legacy in disarray. It could include people who were long admired for what they stood for but toward the end allowed their good reputation to pass behind a cloud. I can think of those who refused to accept retirement because they would not give up the precious ministry they built and hand it over to a younger person. I think of those who became bitter toward the end and left their followers disillusioned. These people may not go to hell, but not finishing well below has repercussions at the judgment seat of Christ above.

Perception Is Reality

It may be unfair, but so often it is true that perception is reality. The way people view you and the way you present yourself is the impression you will leave behind. People will make judgments about your appearance, your attitude, the people you are associated with, the way you use words, your presence of or lack of wisdom, and what people generally *perceive* to be true. It's a cruel world. Like it or not, what people believe to be true is what sticks.

When I pray before speaking, I ask that people's *perception* of what I preach will be grasped and applied as God intends. What I say is one thing; what people perceive that I say is what sticks. So in that sense perception becomes reality.

Dying well therefore partly refers to people's perception of the deceased. The person may finish well in one sense—namely, be personally walking with the Lord, but be perceived as one who will be remembered for other things—such as a sexual or financial scandal, being arrogant, dishonest, imprudent, or unforgiving. Richard Nixon might have finished well in the sense of being personally right with God before he died— insofar as his personal salvation is concerned, but Watergate and his forced resignation of the presidency will forever be etched in people's minds when they think of him.

There are arguably two aspects of dying well:

1. What people think

2. The truth

The good news—or for some not so good news—is that the *truth* will be unveiled at the judgment seat of Christ. "There is nothing concealed that will not be disclosed, or hidden that will not be made known" (Luke 12:2). The truth will come out. The truth—and only the truth—will be vindicated. And whether we have spoken the truth will be made known. Whether we have been genuine or phonies will be exposed. Nothing will be hidden. So I will quote it yet again: "Judge nothing before the appointed time; wait until the Lord comes. He will bring to light what is hidden in darkness and will expose the motives of the heart. At that time each will receive their praise [or lack of it] from God" (1 Cor. 4:5). We will give account for every idle word, my least favorite verse in the New Testament (Matt. 12:36)! For we must all appear before the judgment seat of Christ in order to receive reward or punishment for the things done in the body, whether good or bad (2 Cor. 5:10).

Jesus is called the "righteous Judge" (2 Tim. 4:8). He will not be bribed. No one will manipulate Him. He owes no one a favor. He has nothing to prove. He will be impartial, fair, honest, and governed entirely by what is true.

This teaching is made known to us in Scripture mainly that we might anticipate the final judgment. God did not have to warn us that it is coming. He could have sprung it on us at the last minute. But no. He has given us ample warning: everything will be made known. The truth regarding unsolved crimes. Unjust judgments. Unfair laws. Political favors. Secret affairs. Financial improprieties. Lies. Ruthless ambition. Destroyed reputations. People getting away with murder. Unvindicated integrity. People who suffered without complaining. Unrewarded obedience. What is orthodox, what is heresy. It will all come out on that day of days.

WILL ALL OF OUR PAST—GOOD AND BAD—BE REVEALED AT THE JUDGMENT?

There are two points of view on whether our sins—even those washed by the blood of Jesus—will be revealed:

1. My view, that sins confessed to God and repented of will *never* be revealed.

2. Arthur Blessitt's view, that even sins that have been forgiven will be known.

Arthur asks: Why should David—and other biblical characters who fell—be exposed in Scripture? Why should we be dealt with any differently? My advice: live as though Arthur's view is right; it will do us all good in the present life; then hope that my view is correct; we will all be relieved!

Why is it that not all Christians finish well? A Christian finishing well means that you as a saved person came into your inheritance and pursued it to the end. We have seen above, every Christian is called to come into his or her inheritance. Some do, some don't. Those who do and pursue it, truly finish well. They not only go to heaven; they also receive a reward at the judgment seat of Christ.

CAN A SAVED PERSON EVER BE LOST?

There is not a single verse in the Bible that teaches you can be truly saved and then be eternally lost. All warnings to Christians in Scripture refer to losing one's inheritance, the prize, the crown, or one's reward. When Paul wrote his first letter to the Corinthian Christians, he revealed how eagerly he was pursuing the "prize" or "crown." He even said, "I strike a blow to my body and make it my slave so that after I have preached to others, I myself will not be disqualified for the prize" (1 Cor. 9:27). He did not beat his body to stay "saved." The thought of losing his salvation and incurring the eternal wrath of God was not on his mind at all. He put himself under rigorous discipline—which included keeping himself pure—that he might not lose his reward, something that was very important to him! He wrote 1 Corinthians in AD 55 or 56. He wrote 2 Timothy in AD 67 or 68—very shortly before he went to glory. He was not afraid to assert that "a crown of righteousness" now awaited him (2 Tim.

4:8). It is the same thing as a "rich welcome" into the eternal kingdom (2 Pet. 1:11).

The purpose of this book is to challenge you to finish well—to know you are saved, which is the main thing; and to know you have truly pursued your inheritance—which is what, surely, you and I want to do. As I said, some do, some don't. But all can. Will you?

If you are reading this book it is not too late to finish well, that is, to know you will go to heaven.

Can You Still Finish Well After You Have Seriously Messed Up?

And if you feel you have lost any hope of a reward in heaven, read on. What if you have made a mess of things up to now? Is there hope that you might—from this moment—have a wonderful turnaround and begin today to pursue God's inheritance for you? Yes.

King David sinned as horribly as any person in the Bible. First, he committed adultery. Then he committed murder to cover up the adultery. It would seem that he got away with both for a while. The scholars reckon that it was some two years before Nathan the prophet knocked on his door and exposed David's sin. There is every reason to believe that, had not Nathan intervened, David would have gotten away with both adultery and murder. But he did not get away with either; he was exposed. And dealt with severely from that day forward.

If the only man in Scripture called a man after God's own heart got caught for his sin, who are we that we dare imagine we could get away with these things? David was found out *because* he was special. Why does a living man complain for the punishment of his sins (Lam. 3:39)? Being punished now is better than being punished later. When we are found out in the here and now, it is a sign of mercy. God's loving chastisement. It is being disciplined, yes. But it is sweet compared to what it will be like in the age to come. Those who get away with sins not confessed and repented of will have to face them at the judgment. It will be a thousand times more painful then to have to face the consequences of sin at the judgment seat of Christ. However painful, embarrassing, or inconvenient, it is far better to be found out *now* than to face it before God—with the whole world watching as well.

In my book *The Anointing* I describe King Saul as "yesterday's man."[5] Some have argued that David's sin was surely worse than Saul's. David committed adultery and murder, breaking two commandments of the moral law. Saul went against the details of the ceremonial law, then later would not destroy all the Amalekites as God ordered. Apart from examining the details of these men's sins, the huge difference is that King Saul was defensive and unrepentant; David was immediately sorry and accepted everything Nathan said. Saul completely blew away his inheritance. So did David—up to then. But because David repented he was given a second chance to show his desire to please God.

Let us say you have messed up—hugely. Equal to what either Saul or David did. The question is, will you defend yourself? Or will you accept God's verdict? Had not Saul defended himself but confessed his folly immediately, he would have had a future. But he defended himself, claiming he felt "compelled" to go right against Holy Scripture (1 Sam. 13:12). As a consequence of his unteachable and inflexible self-defensiveness, King Saul was never granted repentance. He became like those described in Hebrews 6:4–6; they were illuminated by the Spirit, they tasted the word of God, were partakers of the Holy Spirit and the powers of the world to come. Something went badly wrong for them, however. In my view those described in this passage were truly saved but not able to be renewed *again* to repentance. They were never again to be changed "from glory to glory." They became yesterday's men and women. It is my opinion, therefore, that Saul had been converted, for he had been given a new heart (1 Sam. 10:9). But he irrevocably blew away his inheritance by his unrepentant stance.

There are two kinds of yesterday's men or women. First, there are those who are put on the shelf and forced to give up their positions. This is humiliating. But such people have a future if they will climb down from their arrogance, truly repent—and learn. Second, there are those yesterday's men and women who carry on with their ministries without any slowing down. They won't take the wisdom of people to whom they should be accountable. They refuse to climb down. They are not at first seen as yesterday's men; like King Saul, who carried on for another twenty years, they hold on to their followers, and nobody knows they are yesterday's men or women. As in the case of King Saul, only God knows the truth about them (1 Sam. 16:1).

Is there a second chance for those who blew away their inheritance?

David repented with all his heart and soul. He did not shed crocodile tears for public show and sympathy. He was totally distraught before Nathan and God. It would be a long haul, but he had a future. Best of all, he could pursue his inheritance and show how much he loved God.

The key to knowing whether you are a *Saul* or a *David* who has fallen is whether you honestly and truly want to get totally right with God *whether or not you get your ministry or position back.* If one's only motive to repent and *get right with God* is to get their previous position back, I fear that it is a feigned repentance. But if one is willing to serve the Lord in humility and faithfulness without getting their position back, such people have a future.

DAVID'S FINEST HOUR

David's finest hour came when he refused to exploit the august presence of the ark of the covenant when he was later in exile. In the meantime God had allowed David to be punished severely, not least was when his son Absalom stole the hearts of the people and David was forced to give up the kingship. The ark, however, had remained with David. He knew of its glory, its significance, its prestige. Some might have even thought it carried divine influence and would protect David and secure his restoration to the throne. But he said to Zadok the priest:

> Take the ark of God back into the city. If I find favor in the LORD's eyes, he will bring me back and let me see it and his dwelling place again. But if he says, "I am not pleased with you," then I am ready; let him do to me whatever seems good to him.
>
> —2 SAMUEL 15:25–26

These words reveal the real David—his integrity, vulnerability, transparency, and love for the glory of God. There is a future for a man or woman like that.

So if you have messed up, whether severely or perhaps less so, be sure that your heart is to bring honor to God and not to make yourself look good. First, there is a future for you—here on earth. Second, you are most certainly building up a reward that will be unveiled at the judgment seat of Christ.

David temporarily blew away his inheritance. But he got it back. So can you.

CONCLUSION

*Therefore, my brothers and sisters, make every effort to con-
firm your calling and election. For if you do these things, you
will never stumble, and you will receive a rich welcome into
the eternal kingdom of our Lord and Savior Jesus Christ.*
—2 PETER 1:10–11

All's well that ends well.
—WILLIAM SHAKESPEARE (1564–1616)

A CHRISTIAN FINISHING WELL—WHETHER they be a
church leader with a high profile or a humble servant
barely known—will be characterized by certain principles. So
if you want to be sure that you finish well, what follows in this
conclusion, I believe, will guarantee that you finish well.

Paul Stanley and Robert Clinton offer five characteristics of
those who have finished well:

1. They had perspective, which enable them to focus.

2. They enjoyed intimacy with Christ and experienced repeated times of inner renewal.

3. They were disciplined in important areas of life.

4. They maintained a positive learning attitude.

5. They had a network of meaningful relation-
ships and several important mentors during their
lifetimes.[1]

Ten Principles for Finishing Well

In addition to these valid principles, I close with ten of my own:

1. Put yourself totally under Holy Scripture.

Resolve to be governed by Scripture—your theology, your life-style, and in all your decisions of life. "Though it cost you all you have" (Prov. 4:7), submit to Scripture. Therefore wherever it takes you—or whatever it keeps you from doing—put yourself under the teachings of the Bible. Be sure that there is nothing you do privately or publicly that goes against it.

This first principle assumes, however, that you know your Bible! Do you? Do you read it? How often? How much? Do you have a Bible-reading plan? You need a plan. We all do. In 1977 Dr. Martyn Lloyd-Jones introduced me to a plan devised by Robert Murray M'Cheyne.[2] It takes me through the Bible in a year plus the New Testament and Psalms twice. You can go online and get your own one-year Bible-reading Plan. We all need a program that will keep us in the Word of God. A frequent fringe benefit of a plan is that the Holy Spirit will speak to you unexpectedly day after day in a way that shows He is on your case. Furthermore, the Holy Spirit will never speak contrary to the Book He wrote. Also, when you have a Bible-reading plan, you realize that you are not making things happen when the Holy Spirit powerfully applies a verse to you. He knows what your thoughts are and will direct the Holy Spirit to speak to you in an astonishing manner.

But reading it is not enough. Knowing its contents is not enough. You must obey its teachings. This means to put yourself under it. Do not lean on your own understanding (Prov. 3:5). You must bow to Scripture when it comes to decision making.

King Saul's downfall came initially because he put himself above the Word of God. Since Saul was king he reckoned that he was the exception. Believe me, none of us is an exception—whether you are a prophet, theologian, royal, unknown, poor, wealthy, or church leader. Humble yourself. Don't fancy you are exceptional and can bypass Scripture when it comes to how you think and what you do. If you want to be a fool, regard yourself as one who knows better than Scripture what is true and good. When King Saul offered the burnt offerings, he knowingly went against Holy Scripture. The Bible is the infallible Word of God. I would lovingly caution that the moment you begin to doubt this, you set yourself up for an inevitable fall—sooner or later. When Saul said he felt "compelled" to offer the burnt offerings (1 Sam. 13:12), it was tantamount to people saying, "God told me to do this"—knowing full well that they are going against Holy Scripture. Live by the Word of God—all of it—and you are in a good place to finish well.

2. Be accountable to reliable people.

"I'm accountable only to God." Have you ever heard someone say that? I can tell you, they are the famous last words of *yesterday's man*. When a church leader—whether they be priest, pastor, prophet, or preacher—says, "I am accountable *only to God*," it is a pious-sounding way of avoiding being accountable to responsible people. Nobody is so spiritual that he or she does not need to be accountable to reliable people who will speak truthfully. The best proof that you are truly accountable to God is that you *volunteer to be accountable to good people around you.*

That said, one must be on their honor to do this. One can claim to be accountable and still be living a double life. You, then, must be honest and open to trusted friends. I thank God for friends who are not afraid to tell me what I don't want to hear. King Saul was supposed to be accountable to Samuel. But he wasn't.

One of the greatest shocks and disappointments of my life was when a man who asked to be a member of Westminster Chapel stopped returning my phone calls. I knew something was wrong. He claimed to be accountable to us. But he wasn't. I lovingly warned him, "I am afraid you are going to become yesterday's man." Two years later we found out that he had been living a double life.

You can say you are in an accountability group, and it may sound good, but being in the group is not enough. You must become vulnerable and play by the rules—to hide nothing from them when they could help you. Therefore one is truly accountable only to the degree he or she is *willing* to be accountable by being transparently honest about one's private life, marriage, finances, and temptations. We all need friends who know where we are at any time, what our hurts and vulnerabilities are.

3. Be squeaky clean regarding finances.

This means more than paying your bills on time or avoiding debt—as essential as those are. Being squeaky clean means more than living within your income, essential though this is. Neither is it enough merely to tell the truth to your accountant or the IRS. The importance of these surely goes without saying.

Jesus had more to say about money than any other subject! The Sermon on the Mount has a lot to say about money. If we seek first the kingdom of God and His righteousness, God will take care of the essential needs—food, shelter, and clothing (Matt. 6:33).

There are two verses closely connected to this issue. First, remember that worldliness consists of "the lust of the flesh, the lust of the eyes, and the pride of life" (1 John 2:15). Worldliness is craving what money can buy so you can impress people with what you have. The mishandling of money can be traced to worldliness.

Second, "the love of money is a root of all kinds of evil. Some people, eager for money, have wandered from the faith and pierced themselves with many griefs" (1 Tim. 6:10). Mishandling of money can be traced to the love of money.

Are you willing to let anybody see how you use your money? This does not mean you necessarily need to divulge the amount of your income or wealth. But would you be willing for anyone to know where your money comes from and where it goes? Beware of greed. Guard carefully to keep money designated for a certain project or purpose and make sure it goes exactly where it is supposed to go. Otherwise you will join countless people who did not finish well owing to the love of money.

Be generous. Be strict when it comes to knowing where all the money goes, but be liberal when it comes to giving to God, charities, and the poor. Are you a tither? Those who faithfully and consistently give to God what is His are in a good position to finish well. Let there be no hint of a financial scandal in your business, ministry, or personal life.

4. Maintain sexual purity.

Billy Graham has said that it seems that the devil gets 75 percent of God's best servants through sexual temptation. A Christian leader falls almost every day somewhere in the world. Nothing brings disgrace upon the name of God and the church like sexual immorality does. Nothing brings heartache to one's spouse and children like infidelity when it comes to sex. The world loves to hear it about us! It gives them cause to say we are no different than anyone else when it comes to sexual promiscuity.

Most leaders who do not finish well more often than not owe their failure either to sexual or financial improprieties. Paul said, "But among you there must not be even a hint of sexual immorality, or of any kind of impurity, or of greed, because these are improper for God's holy people" (Eph. 5:3).

I don't think you can be too careful when it comes to the issue of sexual purity. None of us knows how strong we will be in a moment of sudden temptation. The best way to avoid falling into sin is to avoid the temptation. We all know in advance what and who will likely tempt us. Simple advice: don't go there! Make no provision for flesh, "do not think about how to gratify the desires of the flesh" (Rom. 13:14).

This includes pornography—the greatest sin among preachers. The Pharisees assumed themselves keeping the Law if they did not physically commit adultery. But Jesus talked about *lusting after a woman* (Matt. 5:28). A Pharisee could indulge in pornography and feel he had not broken the Law, but Jesus's teaching categorically outlaws pornography. Pornography is not only a counterproductive addiction; it will also destroy you if you do not completely stop it. I urge you to stop it immediately. It is not only unsatisfying, but it is also a habit that will sap your spiritual energy, weaken your character, militate against wisdom, and, if you are married, eventually ruin your marriage.

Do you want to finish well? Stop watching pornography. Are you having an affair or thinking about having an affair? Hear the word of the Lord: Stop it! Break it off now. It is only a matter of time until you would give a thousand worlds to roll back time to this moment.

A huge part of my own finishing well will be that I maintain sexual purity and faithfulness to Louise right to the day I die. Alongside this would be that my children believe in me. I pray they will not merely believe what I teach and preach but also know that I have lived it—to the hilt.

5. Come to terms with jealousy when you feel threatened by another person's gift, anointing, or popularity.

The beginning of King Saul's downfall was rooted in his jealousy of David. He became so jealous that the threat of young David occupied his attention more than the Philistines—the enemy of Israel! It all began after David killed Goliath.

> When the men were returning home after David had killed the Philistine, the women came out from all the towns of Israel to meet King Saul with singing and dancing, with joyful songs and with timbrels and lyre. As they danced, they sang: "Saul has slain his thousands, and David his tens of thousands."
>
> —1 SAMUEL 18:6–7

Oh dear. Things were never the same again. From that moment King Saul kept a jealous eye on David.

People can be so insensitive, especially when they innocently praise another minister to their minister. The average person in the pew has no idea how insecure their pastor is.

Don't beat yourself black and blue if you have a weakness in this area. We all have this weakness; we are all prone to jealousy. But we must come to terms with it. Don't deny it, don't repress. Admit it and refuse to let it dominate you.

Have you thought of praying for the person who is a threat to you? Pray not only for your enemy, but also for the person who threatens you. Don't say, "God, I commit them to you." No. Ask God to *bless* them. Be careful; God may answer your prayer! But here's a promise: you will not only make progress in overcoming jealousy, but the blessing of the Holy Spirit on you will also convince you that it is an unselfish prayer!

6. Be willing not to get the credit for what you do.

As we saw above, this principle is the heart of John 5:44: "How can you believe since you accept glory from one another but do not seek the glory that comes from the only God?" One way of seeking the honor that comes from God only is to make an effort *not* to get the credit for any good we might do alone. We make a choice: either to seek credit from people or seek God's reward.

Mordecai secretly saved the life of King Xerxes. Mordecai accidentally discovered that two of the king's officers were going to assassinate the king. He told Queen Esther that the king's life was in danger. She reported it to the king, giving credit to Mordecai. It was recorded in the book of the annals in the presence of the king. But it was forgotten. Mordecai did not broadcast it. It might even have gone unnoticed. But one night when the king could not sleep, he had the book of the chronicles read to him. When he learned that his life had been spared, he asked whether Mordecai was recognized for this. That is how Mordecai's good deed was discovered. (See Esther 2:21–23; 6:1–3.) It led not only to the defeat of Mordecai's bitter enemy, Haman, but also to the preservation of the Jews.

If God wants to give you the credit for something you did, He will do it.

Everything the Pharisees ever did, whether giving, praying, or fasting, was done solely for people to see (Matt. 6:1–18; 23:5). They were incapable of doing good things and keeping quiet about it. *All* they did was with a view of getting noticed by people.

But more than that, some stick to their guns based upon a theological or political position because their pride is at stake. It is possible to hide behind a valid principle when at bottom it is one's personal pride that is the real reason for one's staunch stand. Caution: hanging on to a valid principle when it has more to do with your ego than the truth is a recipe for not finishing well. It has happened too many times.

The principle that lies behind John 5:44 is possibly the severest challenge to our ego of any in the Bible. We are all innately proud, self-righteous, defensive, and craving recognition. When our ego is truly crucified with Christ, we are in a good place. Maintaining this kind of life guarantees we will finish well.

7. Always keep your word.

Integrity and finishing well are inseparable. We saw that the faithfulness of God is that He keeps His Word. We must mirror the faithfulness of God in our lives—publicly and privately.

King Saul revealed how low a person could sink when he

could no longer keep his word. First, to his son Jonathan. It was not a mere promise that King Saul did not keep; he broke an oath. Not keeping your oath in ancient times was very, very serious. You might be forgiven for not keeping a promise you made to someone, but if you ever swore an *oath*, you would move heaven and earth to keep it. When Jonathan pleaded with his father to stop harming David, "Saul listened to Jonathan and took this oath: 'As surely as the LORD lives, David will not be put to death'" (1 Sam. 19:6). But in no time Saul did everything in his power to kill young David. Later on—twice—when David could have killed Saul but didn't, Saul promised not to harm David again. But he immediately broke his word. Saul's word was not worth anything anymore.

One should not have to swear an oath to guarantee he or she will tell the truth. This was part of Jesus's point in the Sermon on the Mount (Matt. 5:33–37). Telling the truth, keeping our word, honesty in all verbal exchanges is what decent human beings do. And yet it has been known for people to break their word and—in the end—become utterly untrustworthy.

When wanting to know if a person is genuine, I have heard people ask the question, "Is he the real deal?" Or if they say, "She *is* the real deal" it means that person is honest. Real. Pure gold. Not phonies. Not hypocrites.

Maintaining integrity, then, is the guarantee you and I will finish well.

8. Live in total forgiveness.

It is fairly well known among those who have followed my ministry that the Romanian pastor Josef Tson once said to me in the greatest crisis of my life: "RT, you must totally forgive them. Unless you *totally forgive them* you will be in chains.

Release them, and you will be released." No one had ever talked to me like that in my life. "Faithful are the wounds of a friend" (Prov. 27:6, MEV). It was the best word anybody *ever* gave me. It completely changed my life.

The surest way to enjoy the presence of the *ungrieved* Holy Spirit is to avoid all bitterness, stop speaking negatively of people, and totally forgive those who have hurt you or hurled any measure of injustice toward you (Eph. 4:30–32).

Living in unforgiveness is injurious to your health. Not forgiving is to give Satan an entry point. We must forgive so Satan does not "outsmart" us (2 Cor. 2:11, NLT). Holding a grudge is what the devil wants of you. Don't give the devil that pleasure!

Living in total forgiveness means you will tell no one what *they* did to you. You will not intimidate any one. You will help them forgive themselves and refuse to let them feel guilty. You let them save face (as opposed to rubbing their noses in it). You protect them from their darkest secret. Like a pill you might have to take the rest of your life, total forgiveness is a life sentence; you have to keep doing it—literally every day for the rest of your life. Finally, total forgiveness means that you bless them, that is, you pray for them that God will truly bless them. Caution again: God may answer your prayer!

Live this way for the rest of your life. What begins as a gargantuan effort eventually becomes a pleasure. It is almost selfish! The benefits of living like this are so wonderful that you might question your motive for living this way! You will never be sorry—I guarantee it.

9. Be a thankful person.

After I finished my book on thanking God, *Just Say Thanks!*[3], I came upon an interesting statistic: thankful people live longer.

God loves gratitude and hates ingratitude. One of the most important verses is this: "Be anxious for nothing, but in everything by prayer and supplication, *with thanksgiving*, let your requests be made known to God" (Phil. 4:6, NKJV, emphasis added). When I preached on this verse thirty years ago, I was gripped by it in a way I had not anticipated. I preached myself under conviction! It was as though my whole life came up before me. I was made to see how lax I had been over the years in not remembering to be thankful. I made a vow to be a thankful man. From that day to this I have made it a habit to thank God every single day for the various blessings of the previous twenty-four hours.

It takes less than fifteen seconds: thank God for at least three things every day before you go to bed each night.

God notices when we are thankful. I should also say that He notices when we forget to be thankful. On one occasion Jesus healed ten lepers. Only one came back to Him to say "thank you." Jesus's first question: Where are the other nine who were equally cleansed? (Luke 17:17). That is sobering evidence that God notices when we don't thank Him for what He has done.

The biblical doctrine of sanctification can be called the doctrine of gratitude. Sanctification, as we saw earlier, is not what guarantees we will go to heaven; faith in Jesus's blood assures of that. Sanctification—the process by which we become more and more holy—is saying *thank you* to God for saving us. That said, the absence of it is noticed and leads to our impoverishment.

Being a thankful person also makes you a cheerful person and more fun to be around.

10. Maintain a strong personal prayer life; spend much time alone with God.

Many years ago I had the privilege of meeting Richard Wurmbrand (1909–2001), the famed Romanian pastor who suffered considerable physical torture under communism. Interestingly enough he was Josef Tson's mentor. This means Richard Wurmbrand was to Josef what Martyn Lloyd-Jones was to me. Dr. N. B. Magruder, who preached my ordination sermon, introduced me to Mr. and Mrs. Wurmbrand when I was a seminary student. I will never forget Richard Wurmbrand's first words to me: "Young man, spend more time talking to God about men than talking to men about God."

John Wesley used to counsel his preachers that they should spend two hours talking to God for every one hour talking to one another. That is more than I could recommend—or do. But it stresses the way great men of old took personal prayer very, very seriously.

For some reason I have been impacted largely over the years by people who prayed a lot. Beginning with my dad, who was not a minister, those ministers who prayed one to two hours a day were those I wanted to emulate and spend time with.

How much do you pray?

I spent the whole of my time at Westminster Chapel endeavoring to pray two hours every morning—not counting sermon preparation—in quiet time with God. That pattern has continued, as much as I am able, to this present day.

There will be no praying in heaven. Praying is never wasted time.

Finally, Two Things

If I should indeed finish well—always remembering that, "It ain't over till it's over"—I would attribute it mainly to two things: reading the Bible through every year and endeavoring to pray at least an hour alone every day. These two things together are the key for me.

Finishing well is the greatest success of all. What is more: *it is not too late for you to finish well.*

> *May the blessing of God the Father, God the Son, and God the Holy Spirit abide with you all. Amen.*

Notes

Preface

1. R. T. Kendall, *In Pursuit of His Glory* (Lake Mary, FL: Charisma House, 2004).

Chapter 1
Never Too Late, Never Too Early

1. J. I. Packer, *Knowing God* (Westmont, IL: InterVarsity Press, 1993).
2. AmericanRhetoric.com, "I Have a Dream," http://www .americanrhetoric.com/speeches/mlkihaveadream.htm (accessed March 24, 2015).
3. R. T. Kendall, *Totally Forgiving God* (Lake Mary, FL: Charisma House, 2012).

Chapter 2
When God Plays Hard to Get

1. Goodreads.com, "Joyce Meyer Quotes," http://www.good reads.com/quotes/328011-patience-is-a-fruit-of-the-spirit-that -grows-only (accessed March 24, 2015).

CHAPTER 3
THE MYSTERY OF PRAYER

1. *Joni and Friends*, "The Mystery of Prayer," http://www.joni andfriends.org/television/mystery-prayer/ (accessed May 6, 2015).

2. R. T. Kendall, *Did You Think to Pray?* (Lake Mary, FL: Charisma House, 2008).

3. "Sweet Hour of Prayer" by William W. Walford. Public domain.

4. As quoted in Linda Evans Shepherd, When You Don't Know What to Pray (Grand Rapids, MI: Revell, 2010), 12. Viewed at Google Books.

5. As quoted in Adam Stadtmiller, Praying for Your Elephant (Colorado Springs, CO: David C. Cook, 2014), 21. Viewed at Google Books.

6. William Cowper, *Poems by William Cowper*, vol. 2 (Cornhill, England: Manning, Loring and E. Lincoln, 1802).

CHAPTER 4
UNANSWERED PRAYER

1. D. Martyn Lloyd-Jones, *Studies in the Sermon on the Mount* (Grand Rapids, MI: Wm. B. Eerdmans Publishing, 1958).

2. Robert Murray M'Cheyne, *The Works of the Late Rev. Robert Murray McCheyne* (New York: Robert Carter and Brothers, 1874), 138.

3. "Human Trafficking Statistics, Polaris Project, accessed at http://www.cicatelli.org/titlex/downloadable/human%20 trafficking%20statistics.pdf (accessed March 30, 2015).

4. Rick Warren, *The Purpose-Driven Life* (Grand Rapids, MI: Zondervan, 2002).

5. "There Is a Green Hill Far Away" by Cecil F. Alexander. Public domain.

CHAPTER 5
ANSWERED PRAYER

1. The Churchill Centre, "Never Give In," speech given at Harrow School, October, 29, 1941; accessed at http://www .winstonchurchill.org/learn/speeches/speeches-of-winston -churchill/103-never-give-in (accessed March 30, 2015).

CHAPTER 6
THE UNSAVED

1. Billy Graham, *Nearing Home* (Nashville: Thomas Nelson, 2011), 95.
2. R. T. Kendall and Rabbi David Rosen, *The Christian and the Pharisee* (London: Hodder & Stoughton Ltd, 2006).

CHAPTER 7
HEALING

1. In personal communication with the author.
2. R. T. Kendall, *Total Forgiveness* (Lake Mary, FL: Charisma House, 2010).
3. R. T. Kendall, *How to Forgive Ourselves—Totally* (Lake Mary, FL: Charisma House, 2013).
4. R. T. Kendall, *Holy Fire* (Lake Mary, FL: Charisma House, 2014).
5. R. T. Kendall, *The Anointing* (Lake Mary, FL: Charisma House, 2003).
6. R. T. Kendall, *The Thorn in the Flesh* (Lake Mary, FL: Charisma House, 2004).

CHAPTER 8
THE PRODIGAL

1. John Ciardi quote cited in *The Westminster Collection of Christian Quotations*, comp. Martin H. Manser (Louisville, KY: Westminster John Knox Press, 2001).

Chapter 9
Revival

1. D. Martyn Lloyd-Jones, Foreword in P. E. Hughes, *Revive Us Again* (n.p.: Marshall, Morgan and Scott, 1947).
2. D. Martyn Lloyd-Jones, *Joy Unspeakable: The Baptism and Gifts of the Holy Spirit* (Lottbridge Drove, Eastbourne: David C Cook, 1995), 469.
3. From William Carey's historic sermon at a gathering of Baptist ministers in Northampton, England in 1792.

Chapter 10
Ten Seconds Before Midnight

1. Charles Dickens, *A Tale of Two Cities* (London: Chapman and Hall, 1859).
2. Maxim Lott, "Top Ten Deadliest Stretches of Road in America," http://www.foxnews.com/story/2009/02/11/top-ten-deadliest-stretches-road-in-america/ (acessed May 6, 2015).
3. R. T. Kendall, *Once Saved, Always Saved* (London: Hodder & Stoughton, Ltd., 1983).

Chapter 11
The Gospel

1. Goodreads.com, "D. Martyn Lloyd-Jones Quotes," http://www.goodreads.com/quotes/99297-if-your-preaching-of-the-gospel-of-god-s-free-grace (accessed March 31, 2015).
2. Ludwig Feuerbach, *Das Wesen des Christentums* (1841), translated into English (*The Essence of Religions*, by George Eliot, 1853, 2nd. ed. 1881).
3. "Amazing Grace" by John Newton. Public domain.
4. As quoted in Alan Richardson and John Bowden, eds., *The Westminster Dictionary of Christian Theology* (Philadelphia, PA: The Westminster Press, 1983), 545.
5. "The Solid Rock" by Edward Mote. Public domain.

CHAPTER 12
MY LIFE VERSE

1. Rick Warren, *The Purpose-Driven Life* (Grand Rapids, MI: Zondervan, 2002).

CHAPTER 13
VINDICATION

1. Thinkexist.com, "Abraham Lincoln Quotes," http://thinkexist .com/quotation/truth_is_generally_the_best_vindication_against /160805.html (accessed March 31, 2015).

CHAPTER 14
GOD'S PLAN AND CALLING

1. Bill Bright, *Have You Heard of the Four Spiritual Laws?* (Peachtree City, GA: Bright Media Foundation and Campus Crusade for Christ, 2007), http://www.crustore.org/fourlawseng.htm (accessed March 31, 2015).

2. Brainyquote.com, "Saint Augustine," http://www.brainy quote.com/quotes/quotes/s/saintaugus148563.html (accessed March 31, 2015).

CHAPTER 15
FINISHING WELL

1. Jim George, *The Bare Bones Bible Handbook* (Eugene, OR: Harvest House, 2014), 46.

2. Thinkexist.com, "Ralph Waldo Emerson Quotes," http:// thinkexist.com/quotation/hitch_your_wagon_to_a_star/8233.html (accessed March 31, 2015).

3. Woody Allen, *Without Feathers* (New York: Ballantine Books, 1975).

4. When asked why the Methodist movement was so successful, John Wesley answered, "Our people die well"; as cited in

Roy B. Zuck, *The Speaker's Quote Book* (Grand Rapids, MI: Kregel Publications, 2009).

5. Kendall, *The Anointing.*

Conclusion

1. Paul D. Stanley and J. Robert Clinton, *Connecting* (Colorado Springs, CO: NavPress, 2014).

2. "Robert Murray M'Cheyne's Bible Reading Calendar," https://cchmb.org/content/plugins/mcheyne-reading-plan/calendar.pdf (accessed April 1, 2015).

3. R. T. Kendall, *Just Say Thanks!* (Lake Mary, FL: Charisma House, 2005).

EXPERIENCE HIS PRESENCE IN A DEEPER WAY

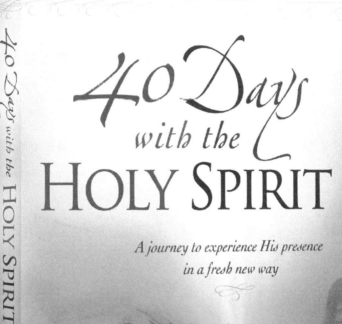

ISBN: 978-1-62136-977-6 | US $14.99

CHARISMA
HOUSE

WWW.CHARISMAHOUSE.COM

SUBSCRIBE TODAY

Exclusive Content

Inspiring Messages

Encouraging Articles

Discovering Freedom

CHARISMA MEDIA

FREE NEWSLETTERS

to experience the power of the *Holy Spirit*

Charisma Magazine Newsletter
Get top-trending articles, Christian teachings, entertainment reviews, videos, and more.

Charisma News Weekly
Get the latest breaking news from an evangelical perspective every Monday.

SpiritLed Woman
Receive amazing stories, testimonies, and articles on marriage, family, prayer, and more.

New Man
Get articles and teaching about the realities of living in the world today as a man of faith.

3-in-1 Daily Devotionals
Find personal strength and encouragement with these devotionals, and begin your day with God's Word.

Sign up for Free at nl.charismamag.com